D1622152

Change in South Africa

CHATHAM HOUSE PAPERS

The Royal Institute of International Affairs, at Chatham House in London, has provided an impartial forum for discussion and debate on current international issues for some 70 years. Its resident research fellows, specialized information resources, and range of publications, conferences, and meetings span the fields of international politics, economics, and security. The Institute is independent of government.

Chatham House Papers are short monographs on current policy problems which have been commissioned by the RIIA. In preparing the papers, authors are advised by a study group of experts convened by the RIIA, and publication of a paper indicates that the Institute regards it as an authoritative contribution to the public debate. The Institute does not, however, hold opinions of its own; the views expressed in this publication are the responsibility of the authors.

CHATHAM HOUSE PAPERS

Change in South Africa

edited by J.E. Spence

The Royal Institute of International Affairs

Pinter Publishers
London

Pinter Publishers Limited
25 Floral Street, Covent Garden, London WC2E 9DS, United Kingdom

First published in 1994

British Library Cataloguing in Publication Data
A CIP catalogue record for this book is available from the British Library

ISBN 1-85567-135-2 (Paperback)
      1-85567-134-4 (Hardback)

DT

1970

C47

1994

Typeset by Koinonia Limited
Printed and bound in Great Britain by
Biddles Limited, Guildford and King's Lynn

CONTENTS

NOTES ON CONTRIBUTORS

Jakes Gerwel is the Vice-Chancellor of the University of the Western Cape. He is the current Chairperson of the Committee of University Principals, chairs the Restructuring Working Group of the recently established National Education and Training Forum and is on the Executive of the ANC's Education Committee. He chaired the Executive Committee overseeing the National Education Policy Investigation conducted by the democratic movement between 1990 and 1992.

William Gutteridge is currently Executive and Editorial Director of the Research Institute for the Study of Conflict and Terrorism (RISCT) in London. He was Senior Lecturer in Commonwealth History and Government at RMA Sandhurst (1949–63), Head of the Modern Studies Department at Lanchester Polytechnic, Coventry (1963–71) and the Complementary Studies and later Political and Economic Studies Group at Aston University (1971–82), where he is now Emeritus Professor. His publications include *The Military in African Politics,* and several titles on South Africa in the *Conflict Studies* series, including 'South Africa – Apartheid's Endgame'.

Michael Savage is Professor of Sociology at the University of Cape Town, where he has been an acting Deputy Vice-Chancellor. He is currently on secondment to the Open Society Foundation for South Africa and is its Executive Director. He is the founding editor of *Social Dynamics* and has research interests in the areas of health, patterns of corporate ownership and control, and race relations.

Olive Shisana obtained her ScD in behavioural sciences from Johns Hopkins University, School of Hygiene and Public Health. For the past

18 years she has been a member of the ANC and was in exile from 1975 to 1991. Upon her return to South Africa she joined the Medical Research Council and is currently Group Manager: Essential Health Research. She has served on a technical committee for the Commission to demarcate South Africa into regions. She is also a member of a think-tank on the Civil Service Policy Project planning a future public service.

Charles Simkins is Helen Suzman Professor of Political Economy at the University of the Witwatersrand. He has degrees from the Universities of Natal and Oxford. He has held positions at the Universities of Natal and Cape Town and has acted as a consultant to the Urban Foundation. He has published widely in the fields of demography, unemployment, income distribution, and housing and urban economics.

J.E. Spence is Director of Studies at the Royal Institute of International Affairs. Born in South Africa, he was educated at the University of the Witwatersrand, Johannesburg, and at the London School of Economics. He has taught at the Universities of Natal, Wales (Swansea) and California, and has held visiting professorships at a number of universities in Southern Africa. He was head of the department of politics at the University of Leicester (1974–81; 1986–91) and Pro-Vice Chancellor (1981–7). Professor Spence is a former President of the African Studies Association of the United Kingdom and Chairman of the British International Studies Association. He was founding editor of the *Review of International Studies* and is an Honorary Fellow of University College, Swansea and the University of Staffordshire.

David Welsh was born in Cape Town and attended the Universities of Cape Town and Oxford. He has taught at the University of Cape Town since 1963 and currently holds the chair of Southern African Studies in the Political Studies Department. He is the author of two books and over one hundred articles, papers and chapters.

ACKNOWLEDGMENTS

The editor wishes to express his gratitude to the following: the contributors to this volume, all of whom responded to the editor's invitation with enthusiasm and commitment; the members of the two study groups which considered the manuscript and whose comments proved invaluable; Margaret May, whose editing skills made a substantial difference to the finished product; Hannah Doe, who dealt with the production; Marie Ciechanowska, who skilfully coordinated the enterprise; and Mary Mileson, who provided secretarial skills of a high order.

January 1994   J.E. Spence

ABBREVIATIONS

ANC	African National Congress
APLA	Azanian People's Liberation Army
AVF	Afrikaner Volksfront
AVU	Afrikaner Volksunie
AWB	Afrikaner Weerstandsbeweging (Afrikaner Resistance Movement)
CODESA	Convention for a Democratic South Africa
COSAG	Concerned South Africans Group
COSATU	Congress of South African Trade Unions
CP	Conservative Party
CSS	Central Statistical Services
ECS	Education Coordinating Services
FA	Freedom Alliance
GATT	General Agreement on Tariffs and Trade
GEIS	General Export Incentives Scheme
GNU	Government of National Unity and Reconstruction
IFP	Inkatha Freedom Party
ISU	Internal Stability Unit
LIBOR	London Inter-bank Offer Rate
MK	Umkhonto we Sizwe (armed wing of ANC)
MPNP	Multi-Party Negotiating Process
NACOSA	National Aids Convention of South Africa
NEPI	National Education Policy Initiative
NETF	National Education and Training Forum
NP	National Party
NPKF	National Peacekeeping Force
OAU	Organization of African Unity

Abbreviations

PAC	Pan Africanist Congress
PWP	Public Works Programme
SACP	South African Communist Party
SADC	Southern African Development Community
SADF	South African Defence Force
TBVC	Transkei, Bophuthatswana, Venda and Ciskei (the 'independent' homelands)
TEC	Transitional Executive Council
UDF	United Democratic Front

Map 1: South Africa

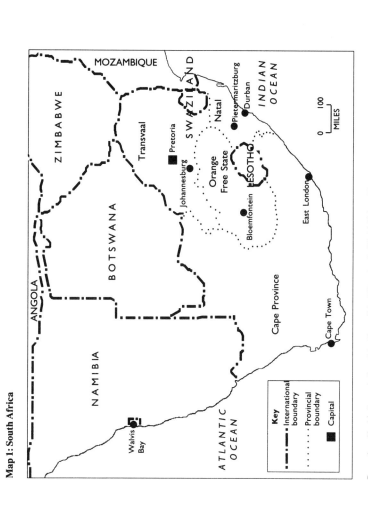

Reproduced by kind permission of the Council for Education in World Citizenship.

Map 2: South Africa's 'Black Homelands'

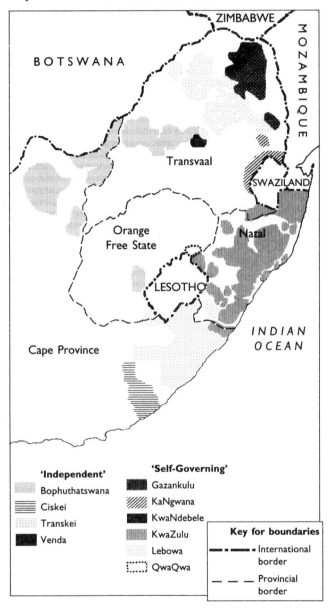

Reproduced by kind permission of the Council for Education in World Citizenship.

1

INTRODUCTION

J.E. SPENCE

The historical context

South Africa's first elections based on universal franchise and proportional representation, on 27 April 1994, represent a defining moment in the country's history, sweeping away the final bastion of apartheid – political discrimination against the black majority. The election is the culmination of three-and-a-half years of tortuous negotiation over the constitution between a variety of political organizations, the most notable of which are President F.W. de Klerk's ruling National Party (NP), the African National Congress (ANC) led by Dr Nelson Mandela, and Chief Mangosuthu Buthelezi's Inkatha Freedom Party (IFP) – a member of the right-wing Freedom Alliance (FA)* – which withdrew from the later stages of the negotiations.

The process began on 2 February 1990, when President de Klerk, in a dramatic and unexpected statement, announced the unbanning of the ANC and other related organizations and the release of Dr Mandela (and other political prisoners) after twenty-six years in prison. What was striking during this period was the enduring strength of the partnership between de Klerk and Mandela and the way in which they steered the negotiation process to a successful conclusion. Indeed, their efforts were rewarded by the award of the Nobel Peace Prize in October 1993.

De Klerk's initiative was rightly perceived as a decisive break with the past. This is true in the sense that his predecessors had always

*This consists of the Conservative Party, led by Dr Ferdi Hartzenberg; the Afrikaner Volksfront, led by ex-General Constand Viljoen; Chief Mangosuthu Buthelezi's Inkatha Freedom Party and President Lucas Mangope and Brigadier Joshua Gqozo, the leaders of the Bophuthatswana and Ciskei homelands.

1

baulked at the idea, for example, of releasing Nelson Mandela and unbanning the ANC, despite considerable pressure from within and beyond South Africa, for fear of the unexpected consequences. De Klerk's speech effectively signalled to his followers and the international community that a 'new deal' was on offer, one which would transform the structure and process of the South African political system. What must be stressed, however, is that the enterprise had its intellectual and political origins in the haphazard reform process that began in the aftermath of the Soweto disturbances in 1976.* The debate these events provoked within the National Party between the *verligtes* (liberals) and the *verkramptes* (hardliners) led to piecemeal reform in the early 1980s during P.W. Botha's term of office as Prime Minister and subsequently President: trade union rights were extended over time to the black majority; so-called 'petty' apartheid laws in the social sphere were relaxed; the policy of job reservation was gradually eased; and Indian and Coloured minorities were incorporated into a tricameral parliament in 1984 side by side with their white counterparts.

De Klerk's predecessors in the *verligte* camp had implicitly recognized that the old Verwoerdian order based on 'separation in all the spheres of living' could no longer be sustained; that reform – however ill-defined as regards long-term objectives – was essential. What de Klerk in effect did was to confront directly the critical issue of black enfranchisement via the mechanism of a new constitutional dispensation. To that extent, then, his February 1990 speech set a radically new agenda, even though its context was influenced by previous reforms, by the fortuitous coincidence of a more favourable international climate and by a variety of domestic constraints which could no longer be ignored.

To begin with, the Botha reforms had had unexpected consequences. Black expectations rose but were dashed when the National Party government refused to legislate for the unenfranchised black majority, insisting throughout that South Africa was threatened by a 'total onslaught' orchestrated from Moscow, with the banned and exiled ANC acting as the spearhead. Hence the enhanced role given to the military in decision-making via the powerful State Security Council and the elaboration of a complex National Management Security System that was designed to provide a vital source of intelligence on black political activity and at the same time – on the 'hearts and minds' principle of counterinsurgency – to

---

*These disturbances were provoked by the government's decision to insist on Afrikaans as the medium of instruction in black schools. This was essentially a revolt by young township blacks, many of whom fled South Africa to join the ANC in exile.

improve the social and economic conditions of the black townships in the urban and rural areas.

This strategy failed to deter the emergence in 1983 of the United Democratic Front (UDF) – a multi-racial alliance of civic organizations created to oppose the promulgation of the 1984 constitution and whose activities provoked the declaration of a state of emergency in July 1985. This was quickly followed by the imposition of 'private' and public sanctions as overseas investors withdrew from South Africa and a variety of international organizations (the European Community, the Commonwealth and the United Nations), together with Western governments – acting with varying degrees of reluctance – attempted to persuade the Botha government to accelerate the reform process then under way.

This combination of events led to prolonged domestic crisis in the late 1980s; the stalemate between the Botha government and the black opposition seemed unbreakable, as the former lacked the will, if not the means, to repress its black opponents into permanent extinction; by contrast, the UDF and its allies abroad (the ANC in particular) could not topple the state, whether by mass demonstration and protest or by armed struggle. But, as the historian H.A.L. Fisher reminds us, 'the play of the contingent and the unforeseen in the development of human destinies'[1] had its role as well: in this case the fortuitous removal of P.W. Botha from the political scene in July 1989, as the result of debilitating illness, and his replacement as State President by the more flexible de Klerk in September 1989.

By the end of 1990 it was clear that the Cold War was over: the Soviet Union could no longer be regarded as a significant threat to the Republic, and the traditional prescription of a 'total strategy' to counter a 'total onslaught' from Moscow was patently absurd. De Klerk gave a hint of what was to come with his virtual abolition of the National Security Management System and the downgrading of the influence of the State Security Council. His task was also eased by the lack of hostile public reaction to South Africa's withdrawal from Namibia and the achievement of that territory's independence in 1990. Hitherto, fear of a white right-wing backlash had served as a powerful constraint on government efforts to meet Western demands for conciliation on the Namibian issue.

Yet another factor was the incentive for change provided by the deepening crisis of the South African economy and de Klerk's recognition that the price of economic recovery was major political reform, especially given that this recovery depended on a revival of trade and investment links with Western states.

3

Figure 1(a): South African population by racial group, 1991

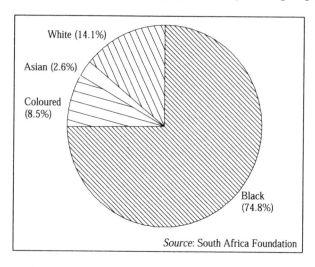

White (14.1%)

Asian (2.6%)

Coloured (8.5%)

Black (74.8%)

Source: South Africa Foundation

Figure 1(b): Distribution of black populations in South Africa, 1991

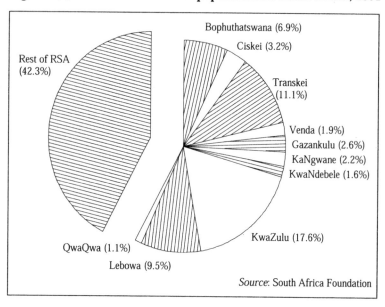

Bophuthatswana (6.9%)

Ciskei (3.2%)

Rest of RSA (42.3%)

Transkei (11.1%)

Venda (1.9%)
Gazankulu (2.6%)
KaNgwane (2.2%)
KwaNdebele (1.6%)

KwaZulu (17.6%)

QwaQwa (1.1%)

Lebowa (9.5%)

Source: South Africa Foundation

Reproduced by kind permission of the Council for Education in World Citizenship.

There was, too, the related pressure of demographic growth: in 1990 South Africa's population was 38.1 million; by 2000 the figure will be 47.5 million (see Figure 1 for a breakdown of the population groups). Providing even a modest level of subsistence and employment for numbers on this scale would require a growth rate of 3–4 per cent. Hence economic revival and political reform went hand in hand. De Klerk also recognized that maintaining the status quo would ultimately be self-defeating: better to negotiate a 'new deal' with the black majority leaders from a position of relative strength rather than wait until the continued pressure of economic decline, growing black militancy and external pressures produced a revolutionary outcome in which white interests would be damaged beyond repair.

Finally, the elusive factor of personality needs to be taken into account: de Klerk was, in his time as a cabinet minister in the Botha government, on the right rather than the left of the political centre of the National Party. Nothing he did as a minister prepared his followers for the *volte face* of 2 February 1990. He had, for example, never held high office in a major ministry concerned with defence, internal security or foreign policy, and few clues were, therefore, forthcoming about the line he might take on South Africa's future once in office. In this context he bears comparison with right-wing leaders such as Charles de Gaulle and Richard Nixon. Unencumbered by ideological baggage of a narrowly restricting kind, both were able to display a masterly understanding of what had to be done in difficult circumstances and were in any case more interested in the exercise of power and the imperatives of national survival than in grandiose objectives of a millennial kind.

The principal of 'cometh the hour, cometh the man' may, therefore, seem an apt description of de Klerk's emergence as white South Africa's 'man of destiny'. It is, however, worth reflecting that the emergence of a strong leader with sufficient determination to break the mould of forty years of apartheid repression was rarely considered a likely option when debate occurred during the 1970s and 1980s on rival theories of social change in South Africa. There were those, especially in the business community both at home and abroad, who placed their faith in the slow inevitable erosion of Verwoerdian apartheid via the mechanism of economic growth; there were others who argued that even the limited reforms of the Botha era would have unforeseen consequences, especially in the political sphere. Finally, there were the advocates of external pressure, in particular the imposition of economic sanctions. It would be foolish to attempt to weigh up the precise role played by each of these factors in producing the transformation of the 1990s: all that can be said with certainty is that their combination, rather than their separate impact, provides the most plausible explanation for the emergence and ultimate success of a new breed of leader in de Klerk and his young lieutenants in the National Party.

The negotiating process

David Welsh's contribution to this volume (Chapter 2) provides a detailed account in which the twists and turns of the negotiations are clearly analysed. It seems appropriate, therefore, to emphasize themes which might be regarded as having some significance both during the transition to a new government and, more importantly, during the period thereafter.

Without a willing negotiating partner, de Klerk's grand initiative would have quickly foundered. He – and indeed South Africa – was fortunate that the newly released Nelson Mandela was prepared to recognize that a constitutional settlement would have to be one which deferred to the need to protect the interests of the white minority and, at the same time, to meet the legitimate and mounting expectations of the black majority. Some of the groundwork of the constitution was, in fact, laid during the last phase of Mandela's imprisonment when a series of cabinet ministers (including P.W. Botha) held discussions with him over the scope and nature of the transition to a new political system, as well as the principles deemed appropriate to underpin it. De Klerk's task was made easier by Mandela's willingness to draw a veil over the iniquities of the past and by his implicit repudiation of the armed struggle as a means of seizing power. Moreover, both leaders took considerable risks as step by step they consolidated their partnership in constitution-building. Throughout the process each presided over divided constituencies; the white right wing – despite its division into a motley collection of some eighty organizations of varying degrees of political effectiveness and popular support – remained bitterly opposed to the concept of negotiation, let alone an outcome which promised an end to exclusive white rule.

The right's capacity to derail the process was demonstrated by the outcome of the Potchefstroom election in February 1992, when the Conservative Party scored an unexpected victory, one which led de Klerk to call a referendum the following month. A total of 68.5 per cent of white opinion endorsed the negotiation process, but nonetheless right-wing sentiment remained vocal, culminating in the formation of the

Freedom Alliance in early 1993. Moreover, de Klerk had to contend with the defection of Buthelezi's IFP – hitherto regarded as the National Party's informal ally in any future new government – because of fierce disagreement over the apparent failure of the multi-party Negotiating Forum to give sufficient weight to the federal principle in the drawing up of the new constitution. Indeed, Buthelezi contended that the NP/ANC axis was bent on marginalizing his movement and his claim to speak for a substantial proportion of the black population. Finally, de Klerk's National Party became progressively demoralized as support drained away to the Conservative Party and its parliamentary caucus realized that only a minority of its members could hope to sustain a parliamentary career in a post-apartheid South Africa.

For Mandela, too, the task of holding the ANC together has proved formidable. One of his closest lieutenants, Oliver Tambo (a prominent member of the so-called 'old guard' and leader of the ANC in exile), died, while the murder of Chris Hani* in April 1993 threatened for a brief moment to undo the progress that had been made so laboriously in the preceding three years. Then again, the young disaffected comrades in the urban townships require constant reassurance that their interests are not being 'sold out' for the sake of accommodation (often interpreted as appeasement) of white minority susceptibilities. There is, too, the role of the South African Communist Party, many of whose leaders occupy positions of authority within the ANC hierarchy and are often accused of having a hidden agenda (once the transitional phase of the so-called 'national' revolution had passed). Their most prominent spokesman, Joe Slovo, was nonetheless (as Welsh stresses) instrumental in persuading the ANC leadership to accept a power-sharing formula as the basis for the first post-apartheid government.

Moreover, once unbanned the ANC had to face the difficulties involved in transforming itself from a liberation movement into a political party able to engage in the humdrum task of mobilizing support, and regional and local organization. Many of the exiles, some 20,000 in all, found it hard to adapt to homecoming, while those who belong to Umkhonto we Siswe (MK, the military wing of the ANC) had no prospect in the short term of absorption into a reconstituted South African Defence Force. (In this context the conclusions of William

---

*Chris Hani, the secretary-general of the South African Communist Party, was the victim of a right-wing plot organized by Clive Derby-Lewis, a prominent member of the Conservative Party, and Janusz Waluz, both of whom were found guilty of Hani's murder.

Gutteridge in Chapter 3 on the composition and role of the new state's security forces are especially relevant.)

As Welsh demonstrates, the negotiation process was marked by periodic breakdowns, mutual recrimination and profound uncertainty about its outcome. Thus in June 1992, for example, the CODESA (Convention for a Democratic South Africa) talks broke down because of deadlock on the scope, structure, role and durability of the proposed interim government, and any resumption of the negotiations in the short term proved impossible following the Boipatong massacre* on 17 June.

Marina Ottaway has perceptively and succinctly summarized the constraints operating upon the negotiation process during this phase:

> Fundamental disagreement remained on the meaning of negotiations and its legal framework, on what had to be negotiated, and on the transitional institutions and the timetable of the process. The climate surrounding the negotiations was poor, with suspicion and anger growing within the ANC ... The ANC still insisted that the National Party give up power quickly to an interim government and that a constitution be enacted later by an elected constituent assembly. The government remained adamant that no transfer of power should take place until a full-fledged, although supposedly transitional, constitution had been negotiated among the CODESA participants and enacted by the existing Parliament.[2]

Yet negotiations did get under way again in December 1992 and continued until their successful conclusion in November 1993. What prevented irretrievable collapse both in June 1992 and March 1993 was the willingness of both the major protagonists, de Klerk and Mandela, to use the resources of private, informal diplomacy ('talks about talks') and to engage jointly in astute crisis management when events threatened to get out of hand. That both felt obliged on occasion to accuse each other of bad faith is unsurprising; neither, given the volatility of their respective constituencies, could afford to be seen to be bedding down too comfortably with the other. A further incentive to keep the enterprise under way was provided by external pressure from the UN and Western governments, together with growing apprehension at the economy's continuing decline – a point brought home by Derek Keys, the National

---

*On this occasion 48 people died as the result of a clash between hostel dwellers and squatters in Boipatong. The hostel was alleged to be a stronghold of the Inkatha Freedom Party.

Party Finance Minister, in briefings to ANC leaders. There was, too, the clear recognition that the process itself was irreversible: there was simply no alternative to a negotiated settlement and far too much was at stake for either of the chief actors to risk defeat and humiliating repudiation at the hands of their followers.

To describe the eventual outcome – the signing of the draft interim constitution in November 1993 – as the triumph of hope over experience would be a half-truth at best: hope there has always been, but South Africa's negotiators, de Klerk and Mandela in particular, had over the years learned from experience that compromise was essential if hope was ultimately to be translated into reality. Twenty-two political parties signed the draft, but the final agreement was, in effect, the product of a complicated deal between the National Party and the ANC. David Welsh examines this deal in detail and has rightly focused on the power-sharing arrangements and the degree to which the 'federal' elements can satisfy the principle of 'unity in diversity'. After all, what the negotiating elites have been struggling to do is to transform a South African state and society within existing national boundaries and thus avoid the violent ethnic fragmentation which has characterized the end of repressive governments and the initiation of a reform process in countries such as the former Yugoslavia and Soviet Union.

During the negotiations it was Chief Buthelezi's predominantly Zulu-based IFP and its Afrikaner allies in the Freedom Alliance which delayed agreement, as the NP/ANC axis tried to meet the former's claims for much greater regional autonomy and the latter's for recognition of the Afrikaners' right to self-determination. Both sides in this debate have cited the break-up of the Soviet Union and Yugoslavia as evidence in support of their case. The ANC, for example, stressed the crucial need to devise a framework which would contribute to effective nation-building and draw heavily on its long-established commitment to promoting non-racialism and the rejection of exclusive black ethnicity as a basis for political struggle and political solution.[3] By contrast, the Freedom Alliance backed its claim to a 'confederal' outcome with dire warnings of the disasters that would follow any attempt to centralize power in the new political system.

Hence the significance of the power-sharing principle; this is at the heart of the new constitution, representing as it does an attempt to involve both majority and minority parties in decision-making. It was the product of a major and profoundly significant compromise between de Klerk's desire to protect the interests of the white minority and the traditional aspiration of the ANC for straightforward majority rule. De Klerk, for all his pragma-

9

tism, has never wavered from his commitment to a constitutional structure in which the white and other minorities would be guaranteed a share in decision-making; initially, he had hoped for an elaborate revolving executive shared between the parties, and a precisely specified blocking mechanism – that is, a percentage (e.g. 60 per cent) of the cabinet's total membership, which would operate if legislation hostile to minority parties was proposed. In the event the constitution provided only for the achievement of cabinet consensus to authorize legislation; this was a major concession by the National Party to meet an earlier concession by the ANC in initially accepting the principle of power-sharing.

Indeed, ANC acceptance of this principle amounts to a recognition that a new government will be hard-pressed to try to satisfy rapidly rising social and economic expectations. It will also have to deal with a civil service and a security force which is predominantly white and conservative. Therefore, a ministry of all the talents combining in a grand coalition is seen as having the necessary authority to impose its will on the civil service and the security forces. At the same time is must be sufficiently broadly based – so it is argued – to take any necessary unpopular measures should expectations get out of hand. This may strike many as a realistic admission of the problems that will face the new state, but it does have serious implications for the protection and assertion of civil liberties in a society in which opposition to tough economic and social policies might well be widespread.

This attempt to institutionalize power-sharing and base it on consensus is significant for two reasons: in effect, the parties have agreed to a 'division of the spoils',[4] a distribution of decision-making power prior to an electoral outcome. It is an attempt to avoid what happened in Angola and elsewhere in Africa when the 'winner takes all' principle operated and the losers refused to accept the result. It is also based on the assumption that the partnership between de Klerk and Mandela, so effective during the negotiation process, can be institutionalized in the new political system: that each, in effect, will accept both the good faith (and the self-interest) of the other in their individual commitment to rule by consensus for the five-year life of the Government of National Unity and Reconstruction.

Clearly, a 'personal' arrangement of this kind places enormous weight on personality and past experience as a guide to future behaviour. What if one or other departs the political scene, for whatever reason? Mandela's ANC is better placed in this context: there are obvious successors waiting in the wings – Cyril Ramaphosa (the Secretary-General of the movement) and Thabo Mbeki (Chairman of the ANC). De Klerk, by contrast, lacks lieutenants of similar stature: those who had obvious claims, such as Barend du Plessis (former Minister of Finance) and Gerrit Viljoen (former Minister of Constitutional Development), have retired and the 'young turks' who led the National Party negotiating team (Roelf Meyer, for example) are not yet obvious candidates for the succession.

Finally, it is worth remarking that the requirements for success in a partnership of the kind that de Klerk and Mandela forged in the negotiating process may well be different once that partnership is locked into government. It is one thing to disagree over major and minor points of constitutional theory and practice, sharing at least a commitment to achieving the end product; it is quite another when matters of high policy are at stake affecting the welfare of constituencies which divide between 'haves' and 'have-nots' with very different expectations of what a new political system can and should deliver.

Coalitions are not easy to run effectively unless there is a single overriding objective, namely the defeat of an external enemy, as was the case in Britain during the Second World War. Clearly, compromise between those who share power after April 1994 will be vital, but far from easy given the immense tasks of social and economic reconstruction that await the new government. Inevitably there will be disagreement about priorities; there will be tension between short-term pressures for immediate amelioration of poverty and deprivation and the longer-term measures required to restructure the economy and generate new resources. Indeed, the magnitude of these related problems is clearly and perceptively spelt out in the contributions of Charles Simkins, Jakes Gerwel, Michael Savage and Olive Shisana in Chapters 4, 5 and 6.

The impact of violence

The legislative enactment of the constitution in late November 1993 by the existing parliament set the stage for the election campaign and the establishment of a multi-party Transitional Executive Council to oversee the day-to-day work of government and supervise the electoral process. This 'watchdog with teeth' (Welsh's phrase) provides a critical test for the capacity of a motley collection of political parties to collaborate – albeit for only five months until the new government is elected – on a power-sharing basis. In particular, the sub-council concerned with overseeing the operation of the security forces may well have to make tough decisions, notably on how best to react to the threat of violence during the elections. There has been much debate about the wisdom of trying to hold elections in a society where the level of violence remains high and some 10,000 people have been killed since 1990.[5] Colin Legum, for example, argued in November 1993 that:

> the four months from the beginning of the election campaign in January to voting day on 27th April, 1994, are likely to be horrendous: a time of political violence, of widespread intimidation, possibly even a white-led rebellion, and acute hostility between the white-led parties, as well as between the predominantly black-led parties.[6]

Thus a heavy burden will be placed on the security forces, although they will have the assistance of monitors and observers from the European Union, the United Nations and the Organization of African Unity (OAU). They, at least, will further help to deter bad behaviour by any individual or party during the campaign. One major difficulty will be the threat of haphazard terrorism by small covert right-wing groups (of which there are many) employing assassination and sabotage – the traditional weapons of the weak who lack the means to topple the state. Prompt action by the security forces will be required to neutralize this threat; clearly the expectation is that the level of violence can be kept to an acceptable minimum.

But even if we assume that the electoral process survives whatever level of violence does occur, and that the election is ultimately pronounced to be 'free and fair', there still remains the danger that violence of the kind that has been a feature of South African politics since the mid-1980s (in Natal) and 1990 (on the Witwatersrand) will remain to damage the new government's best efforts to promote the work of social and economic reconstruction. The root causes of this violence will not be easily extinguished. Moreover, ending the killing will provide a major test of the competence and impartiality of a newly constituted post-apartheid defence force (and in this context Chapter 3, by William Gutteridge, has considerable relevance).

The origins of the violence are complex and cannot be attributed solely to ethnic hostility between, say, Zulu and Xhosa in the Witwatersrand area. In Natal the struggle has involved Zulu against Zulu and is a compound of fierce political competition between Inkatha and the ANC, superimposed on clan rivalries, warlord activity, poverty, growing unemployment and acute competition for scarce resources. It is significant that violence is generally confined to rural and peri-urban areas where 'newcomers' living in shack settlements battle the 'more established' township residents. Equally significant is that unrest is far less widespread in areas where ethnic groups – Zulus, Pondos, Swazi and Xhosas – intermingle and manage a degree of coexistence.

As for the Witwatersrand, it could be argued that the unrest there has had an ethnic dimension as Zulu hostel dwellers, migrating from strife-torn Natal, transfer their hostility, and the political values on which it is based, to an urban context in which the ANC commands wide support among township dwellers. These may well be perceived as belonging to rival ethnic groups, yet Inkatha's opponents do not necessarily define *their* identities in ethnic terms. Belonging to more settled communities, their concerns centre primarily on the politics of deprivation and the struggle to escape the burdens of high rents, poor education and inadequate municipal facilities. Thus, ethnic self-preservation is not necessarily the crucial factor governing their day-to-day relations with hostel dwellers, although tribal antagonism among non-Zulus may surface during attacks or reprisals as opponents are perceived to be exclusively Zulu, armed, dressed and mobilized in glaringly ethnic terms.

In Soweto, for example, 40 per cent of the permanent inhabitants are Zulu, and the evidence suggests that the more settled a community, the less violence there is between members of different ethnic groups. Indeed, much of the violence in the past three years has been between squatters and hostel dwellers, both of whom are recent migrants to urban areas and very often the most deprived in terms of access to township resources. The violence both in Natal and on the Witwatersrand, therefore, has one common feature: it is a struggle among blacks at the bottom of the heap; they seem a world apart from those black elites who have been incorporated into the economic system at a professional level or who have prospects of political or bureaucratic advancement in the new state. This applies particularly to young people, the victims of poor education, unemployment and a crime-ridden culture, for many of whom violence against the security forces and black opponents alike is perceived to be the only available political outlet.

Short- and long-term perspectives on South Africa
Once a new constitutional order is inaugurated, all the parties hope that private and public investors in the outside world – the World Bank and the International Monetary Fund in particular – will be willing to kick-start the South African economy, especially by providing much-needed help to

restore the battered infrastructure of the black rural and urban areas. Indeed, it is possible that as the deprived majority witness that reconstruction under way soon after the inauguration of a power-sharing government, then this – apart from creating much-needed employment – may also go some way to satisfying those expectations and lead to a reduction in the level of violence. John Carlin has a telling vignette which illustrates what is at stake: he quotes a Port Elizabeth ANC leader on the political implications of the appalling shortage of water in black townships:

> If you want to build up a constituency, if you want to get the people on your side, don't talk to them only about freedom and the oppressor and a constituent assembly and all that. That means nothing to them. But tell them you will fight to get them water, and then get it – get them another tap installed – and they will follow you to the ends of the earth.[7]

External private investors will, however, be cautious: they will need to be convinced that the new political system is durable and underpinned by proper economic structures. Thus a dilemma remains: the political stability required for South Africa's reincorporation into the world economy depends in large part on satisfying popular expectations in the short term; yet such external assistance as may be available to help the local economy revive in order to meet those expectations is unlikely to be forthcoming in the short run, just when it is most needed. The principle of 'wait and see' will operate, and help may well be deferred until it is too late to be effective. Of course, it could be argued that whatever the domestic outcome, South Africa cannot expect massive investment inflows. There is, after all, a scarcity of capital in the international political economy and the competition for that scant resource will be intense. Nonetheless, South Africa is better placed than many Third World states to enter that competition. It has economic and physical resources, raw materials and foodstuffs that are still in demand in overseas markets; there is, too, a relatively well-developed infrastructure and an experienced and hardworking business community.

South Africa has traditional trading and investment links with a variety of Western countries. There is, too, the intangible factor that the competing elites share a sense of belonging to the same country and desperately want an outcome which will bury the past and promote the dignity and welfare of all South Africans. This is a necessary, though not a sufficient, condition for a decent outcome.

We must ask, too, whether there is an embryonic human rights culture in South Africa that is sufficiently strong to flourish in due course. There is doubt in some quarters about whether Western-style democracy can take root in an ethnically diverse society such as South Africa's. And perhaps the experience of what is happening in the former Yugoslavia and the former Soviet Union strengthens that scepticism. Yet South Africa does have advantages which many of its counterparts elsewhere on the continent lacked when they became independent: it has a tradition of parliamentary government, albeit a limited one; and it has a judicial system which has produced judges and lawyers of high quality, even if they have very often had to cope with laws which are obnoxious in their treatment of individuals.

Finally, those who govern South Africa after April 1994 are aware of the immense tasks that lie ahead. They know, too, that failure over the long run will mean a precarious slide into Bosnian-style conflict as overpopulation, diminishing resources and political cleavage combine to produce a climate of instability which no amount of external intervention, or remaining vestiges of goodwill at home, will dissipate. The alternative outcome, sometimes posited, is uncontrolled urbanization as black people stream to the cities. Living in burgeoning squatter camps (the Latin American parallel is relevant here), they would not be the stuff of which revolution is necessarily made. They would, however, be a telling symbol of the state's inability to cope.* Whatever the outcome, the outside world might in these apocalyptic circumstances simply write off South Africa as just one more insoluble problem on a troubled and intractable global agenda. The stakes are, therefore, very high.

Regional prospects

What regional role is the 'new' South Africa likely to play? The post-apartheid government is likely to join the Southern African Development Community (SADC), but its impact remains an issue of keen debate. What is certain is that the region's future will, to a large extent, depend on what happens in South Africa under a post-apartheid government. On the assumption of a stable polity and a revived economy, optimists argue that South Africa could become the 'engine of growth' for the entire region: thus capital and technical assistance would be readily available to

---

*In this context, we should note the squatter takeovers in December 1993 of houses in Cato Manor, Durban, set aside for Indian occupation, and of 276 council houses in Mitchells Plain in Cape Town.

help develop the region, while increased trade would produce benefits for all. Achieving this, however, will not be easy. According to Gavin Maasdorp and Alan Whiteside, 'the value of intra-SADC trade is approximately 4% of the total trade of SADC countries; 25% of total trade is with South Africa ... There is a severe imbalance in trade between South Africa and the region: 5.5:1 in favour of South Africa.'[8]

Pessimists claim, however, that the new South African government will be so absorbed in the task of internal social and economic reconstruction that there will be little by way of investment to spare for the country's poorer neighbours. If the new political system breaks down under the pressure of the economic demands made upon it, the region will languish, lacking the stimulus which might otherwise result from a prospering South Africa. Moreover, the danger exists that South Africa will always put its own, rather than the region's, interests first, and these will not always coincide.

However, a third view – that held by the ANC – assumes that South Africa will exercise restraint and sensitivity in its relations with its neighbours, if only to avoid accusations that the new government, like its predecessor, is bent on dominating the region by virtue of its superior economic and political muscle. Indeed, this is Nelson Mandela's view:

> Southern Africa will ... only prosper if the principles of equity, mutual benefit and peaceful cooperation are the tenets that inform its future. Reconstruction cannot be imposed on the region by external forces or unilaterally by ourselves as the region's most powerful state. It must be the collective enterprise of southern Africa's people. Democratic South Africa will, therefore, resist any pressure or temptation to pursue its own interests at the expense of the sub-continent.[9]

Not surprisingly, some of the leaders of the smaller states in the region are apprehensive about the impact of their powerful neighbour on their economic and political systems. They acknowledge the good intentions of the putative new government, but recognize that clashes between 'interest' and 'sensitivity' may occur. For example, by virtue of its superior economic opportunities, South Africa may be a magnet for 'intellectual migrants' from poorer states: doctors, engineers, professionals of all kinds with skills in short supply throughout the region. South Africa might well welcome such talented individuals, but this would surely be a significant source of concern to governments facing the loss of valuable human resources.* Equally, a post-apartheid government might – under pressure from the trade unions – wish to halt the entry of unskilled work-seekers from neighbouring states.

Yet whatever the outcome in the short term, the removal of apartheid and the establishment of a democratic regime will eliminate a major and traditional source of friction between South Africa and the SADC states. There will, at last, be the prospect of normal and straightforward relations, although not necessarily based on an automatic harmony of interests of the kind that some observers have predicted. These relations will contain elements of both conflict and cooperation and, hopefully, be comparatively free of ideological tension – depending on the issue at stake and the extent to which it is a matter of crucial national interest.

Southern Africa and the world

The isolation characteristic of South Africa's position in the international community during the 1970s and 1980s began to break down gradually as the reform process gathered momentum after February 1990. Sanctions were finally lifted in October 1993 and sports and cultural links have been resumed, but well before that date trade missions from Western Europe, Japan and the Middle East began to explore the prospects for profitable ventures in the Republic. At the same time debate began over the degree of association South Africa might enjoy with the European Union, although this is not likely to be settled until the new government takes office in May 1994. South Africa will almost certainly rejoin the Commonwealth, from which it was forced to withdraw in 1961 because of the apartheid policy.

But the world which the new South Africa will enter is a hazardous one: the end of the Cold War has not yet produced a 'New World Order' but rather a 'time of troubles' (Arnold Toynbee's phrase) as the disintegration of communist regimes in Eastern Europe and the former Soviet Union has led to violent and still unresolved conflict. Preoccupation with economic recession and intractable problems of foreign policy closer to home have led the Western powers in particular to downgrade the claims of the Third World for a redistribution of resources in its favour. One consequence is that large parts of Africa are in danger of becoming marginalized.

How will Southern Africa fare in these circumstances? All the states in the region have a powerful incentive to avoid being consigned to the

*See Chapter 6 for amplification of this point.

periphery of the international community, but this assumes that their leaders can and will press ahead with the task of closer economic and ultimately political integration. A thriving regional bloc embracing the states of Southern Africa will at least have some prospect of competing with its counterparts in the northern hemisphere, provided there is a capacity to harmonize economic policies in the interests of the region as a whole rather than operate on the basis of narrow sectional interest. This also assumes that South Africa can and will encourage investment and trade with its poorer neighbours and help in the process of rebuilding the war-battered economies of Angola and Mozambique.

Obviously, Western governments will have an interest in a stable, developing region, one which holds out the prospect of a degree of integration. Indeed, the new South Africa and its neighbours will have a similar interest if only because one important dimension of the so-called 'New World Order' may well be the emergence of powerful trading blocs based on NAFTA (North American Free Trade Association), the European Union and an Asia-Pacific grouping. To survive in that cut-throat world, states in the south will have to seek security and economic advantage by forging closer ties with neighbours. In this respect, Southern Africa may be better placed than other regions in the Third World.

Nonetheless, closer integration will proceed only slowly, along functional lines: transport, water resources and power are three areas where there is scope for regional cooperation, and the hope is that in time multilateral institutions crossing boundaries will emerge to bind the economies of the region closer together. But for this to succeed, South Africa itself, as the most powerful state, will have to prosper and at the same time acknowledge the fears and the aspirations of its neighbours.

Western governments may well encourage this process, but there is a limit to what they can do. South Africa will be perceived as having the primary responsibility for promoting regional linkages and enhancing existing ones; but if these efforts fail because no *local* solutions can be found for the deep-rooted economic and political ills affecting the region as a whole, there will be a real risk of marginalization. Band-aid diplomacy will result, with Western governments scrambling to protect their assets in the region as best they can (e.g. securing the safety of the 800,000 UK passport-holders in South Africa). States in the region have every incentive to avoid such an apocalyptic development.

The road to closer integration will be long and hard; its success depends on so many variables pulling in the same direction to maximize a favourable outcome. Thus the following, *inter alia*, are required:

- A stable economic and political order in South Africa itself;
- The creation of competent and legitimate governments in Angola and Mozambique following the end of civil wars in both states;
- The capacity of neighbouring states such as Zambia, Angola, Mozambique and a post-Banda Malawi to survive the pains of 'a second independence', i.e. to meet the demands of structural adjustment programmes and cope with the pressures imposed by conditionality (aid being tied to evidence of good governance);
- The neutralization of any fears that neighbouring states might entertain about the consequences of admitting their powerful neighbour to existing structures such as SADC.

Moreover, the experience of West European governments will make them cautious about encouraging integration. It will be assumed that Southern Africa will have to find its own road to regional salvation. After all, the EC took over forty years of step-by-step functional integration to reach the present plateau on which past achievement jostles with uncertainty about the future. Furthermore, there are decisive differences between the two regions:

- In 1950 there was rough equality of power between three of the original six states which formed the EC – France, Germany and Italy. No one state could, therefore, dominate the emerging community.
- All the EC states shared common values and a commitment to parliamentary democracy and a mixed economy. To what extent is this true in the Southern African region and, if it is not, what has to be done to make it true?
- There was an industrial and social base in Europe – however battered by war – on which to build new and effective economic structures. In the Southern African region the strength of that base is unevenly spread between large and small states and, more pertinently, between richer and poorer states.
- There were the means available to rebuild Europe, namely Marshall Aid, but no one seriously believes that there is any such prospect for the Southern African region.
- Europe had a charismatic and dominant elite led by technocrats such as Monnet and Spaak who were inspired by the theory of functional integration. The South African equivalent of Jacques Delors has yet to emerge!

Southern Africa will, therefore, have to find its own peculiar mode of closer integration taking into account the particular circumstances of the region. External models may provide some guidance but the local actors, in the last analysis, will have to find local solutions. Perhaps integration is a misleading term in the Southern African context and one that is of little use to either the theorist or the practitioner. It does, after all, have connotations of supranational institution-building and we are a long way from that outcome. Just as European integration proceeded step by step, with one structure building on another until Europe was locked together almost by stealth, in the Southern African context one might argue that cooperation will have to proceed at several levels: bilateral, multilateral, functional and building on what already exists.

The new South African government will also be preoccupied with defining a role for itself in the international community as a whole. The Southern African region is clearly the most important arena for the conduct of its foreign policy: historical experience, traditional economic linkages and geographical position dictate no less. But there also exists an aspiration to be an influential power in the wider continent of Africa, and a flurry of diplomatic activity may be expected as the new post-apartheid government attempts to establish political and economic links with the states of East and West Africa and the Arab countries of the Mediterranean littoral. Indeed, the process has already begun. It has been argued, for example, that South Africa is well placed to be the agent of multinational companies seeking to exploit a regional market. Thus according to Tony Hawkins: 'the sub-Saharan market [is] ... worth some $250bn of which South Africa itself accounts for more than $100bn or more than 40 per cent.'[10]

Certainly, South Africa will join the OAU and be expected to make a contribution to reviving the role that Africa can play in a highly competitive and dangerous world. At the same time, South Africa will have little choice but to enhance its economic links with its traditional trading and investment partners in the West and Japan, which are likely to remain the primary sources of imports as well as important outlets for the exports of its raw materials, foodstuffs and manufactured goods.[11] Thus the new government will have multiple roles to play in the international community – a prospect which the demise of apartheid and the isolation it imposed has at least made feasible.

It was, after all, apartheid which focused the world's attention on South Africa for over forty years. Its destruction at the hands of those who have negotiated a new political dispensation has involved skill and determination, commitment and great enthusiasm. Henceforth, South

Africa will be 'just another country' struggling to make its way in an uncertain world, but there are – as black South Africans will emphatically endorse – far worse fates than that.

Notes

The editor wishes to thank the Council for Education in World Citizenship; the University College of Swansea; and the editor of the *Journal of Commonwealth and Comparative Politics* for permission to use material which first appeared under their auspices.

1 H.A.L. Fisher, *A History of Europe*, London: Edward Arnold, 1937, p. v.
2 Marina Ottaway, *South Africa – The Struggle for a New Order*, Washington, DC: The Brookings Institution, 1993, p. 176.
3 NB Nelson Mandela's statement that 'Respect for diversity has been central to the ANC's political credo. As South Africa gears itself for its first democratic election, this tradition will guide our electoral campaign.' Nelson Mandela, 'South Africa's future foreign policy', *Foreign Affairs*, vol. 72, no. 5, Nov./Dec. 1993, p. 88.
4 The phrase is Robin Christopher's (Foreign and Commonwealth Office). I am grateful for his permission to use it.
5 Between 1 September 1984 and 31 August 1993 political violence killed 17,260 people. In the course of 1993 the trend in killings increased from an average of 4.7 to an average of 11.7 a day. The number of policemen killed in the past decade is 1029. *Fast Facts*, South African Institute of Race Relations, no. 10, October 1993.
6 Colin Legum, *Third World Reports*, London, 24 November 1993, p. 1.
7 John Carlin, 'Squatter camps seek taste of freedom', *The Independent*, 15 October 1993.
8 Gavin Maasdorp and Alan Whiteside, *Rethinking Economic Cooperation in Southern Africa: Trade and Investment*, Johannesburg: Konrad-Adenauer-Stiftung, February 1993, p. 9.
9 'South Africa's future foreign policy', op. cit., p. 91.
10 Tony Hawkins, 'Continental Launchpad', *Financial Times Survey*, 18 November 1993.
11 In 1990 the EC accounted for 27.3 per cent of South African exports while the USA (4 per cent), Japan (6.4 per cent) and Africa (6.7 per cent) were the next most important customers. Similarly, the EC (44.7 per cent), the USA (11.4 per cent), Japan (9.8 per cent) and Africa (1.6 per cent) supplied the bulk of South Africa's imports. Sheila Page and Christopher Stevens, *Trading with South Africa: The Policy Options for the EC*, Overseas Development Institute, Special Report, 1992.

2

NEGOTIATING A DEMOCRATIC CONSTITUTION

DAVID WELSH

Introduction

With its legacy of racial domination, acute conflict and pervasive in-equality, South Africa is an unlikely candidate for inclusion in the ranks of democratic states. For almost four years, beginning with State President F.W. de Klerk's historic speech to parliament on 2 February 1990, South Africa has been in the throes of a difficult and tortuous negotiating process. To understand what has happened and the context of present and future developments it is necessary to appreciate why the main antagonists, the National Party and the African National Congress, agreed to seek a negotiated accommodation.

De Klerk recognized that South Africa was approaching 'an absolute impasse'[1] and that apartheid was incapable of reform: it had to be jettisoned. Nelson Mandela, from his prison near Cape Town, expressed alarm at 'the civil strife and ruin into which the country was now sliding'.[2] He was aware also that the armed struggle being waged by the ANC's military wing Umkhonto we Sizwe (The Spear of the Nation) was incapable of toppling the state with its powerful security forces. He was no doubt aware, too, that sanctions, while seriously haemorrhaging the economy, were unlikely to be decisive in forcing the government to the negotiating table.

In short what had happened was one of those rare moments in history when powerful antagonists mutually recognize that their conflict is stalemated and can be continued only at unacceptable cost. The agreement to negotiate did not mean that the conflict would be terminated; merely that it would henceforth be played out in a political forum. Democracy, after all, is essentially a mechanism for managing and arbitrating conflict. Its spirit was captured by the well-known remark of William Porter, the liberal attorney-general of the Cape Colony in 1853, that he 'would rather meet the Hottentot at the hustings, voting for his representative, than meet the Hottentot in the wilds with his gun upon his shoulder.'

Negotiating postures

The ANC and the NP government approached each other from profoundly differing positions. De Klerk initially hoped that his government's incumbency would enable it to determine the pace and scope of the transition, ensuring that whites would remain protected in a new political system. Many in the ANC, on the other hand, believed that the stage was set for the 'transfer of power'. The unfolding of events, however, was to show that the continuing deadlock imposed severe limitations on each organization's ability unilaterally to secure its demands. The NP and the ANC, in truth, were bound together in 'antagonistic cooperation' (Barrington Moore's term[3]) which obliged them to keep negotiating – even if the process were punctuated by breakdowns or troubled by mutual accusations of treachery and bad faith. Many Nationalists retain a mistrust of the ANC, believing it to be intent on obtaining hegemonic control of South Africa and capable of 'backsliding' into some form of socialism. Conversely, many in the ANC deny that the party which enforced apartheid for over forty years has undergone a change of heart. Suspicions that the NP wanted to delay the transformation for as long as possible and that agents of the state were provoking violence in order to weaken the ANC have remained pervasive.

This querulous relationship has been exacerbated by both organizations' awareness that in due course democratic elections would be held. Constitutional negotiations have proceeded simultaneously with an election campaign whose intensity has increased since agreement was reached that South Africa's first democratic elections would be held on 27 April 1994.

In this difficult process the leadership roles of de Klerk and Mandela have been crucial in ensuring that whatever vicissitudes the negotiating process suffered it would not be permanently derailed. Both realized that the alternative to negotiating was civil war. The relationship between the two men began during 1990 on a constructive, even cordial, note, with Mandela praising de Klerk as 'a man of integrity'. Indeed, Mandela revealed later in a letter to his colleagues that he had met de Klerk, that in his view 'we are dealing with an honest man ... we should negotiate with him'.[4] By mid-1991, however, the relationship had deteriorated. To de Klerk's embarrassment, revelations that state sources had funded Inkatha, ostensibly to assist the anti-sanctions campaign, fuelled ANC suspicions of complicity between the NP government and Inkatha in an effort to weaken the ANC. Mandela accused de Klerk of 'conducting a double strategy towards us, because he could not have been ignorant of [the support of Inkatha]'.[5]

Despite de Klerk's vehement denials, Mandela has persisted in accusing him of fomenting violence or of not doing enough to control the security forces who, the ANC are convinced, are implicated in the violence. By mid-1992, after the breakdown of CODESA and the Boipatong killing, Mandela broke off the negotiating relationship and expressed himself angrily: 'Just as the Nazis in Germany killed people because they were Jews, in South Africa de Klerk, the NP and Inkatha are killing people because they are black.'[6] There were no further negotiations for over three months, during which time the two exchanged angry memoranda.

The multi-party negotiating process

Only diplomatic pressure, and Mandela's realization that South Africa's economic situation made a settlement imperative, brought the ANC back to bilateral negotiations. These culminated in the Record of Understanding, signed by de Klerk and Mandela on 26 September 1992. This agreement was brokered by Cyril Ramaphosa, Secretary-General of the ANC, and Roelf Meyer, Minister of Constitutional Development, who have been the chief negotiators of their respective organizations. Ramaphosa and Meyer remained in communication during the bleak period after mid-1992 and also served as critically important conduits for their leaders. Although the two have not become friends, they have developed a good working relationship that has mitigated the consequences of the flare-ups between de Klerk and Mandela.

However important the 'personal chemistry' that develops between negotiators in facilitating the process, what has been crucial in South Africa's case is the realization by both the ANC and the NP government that there is no alternative to a negotiated accommodation. It is this mutual recognition that has prevented derailment of the process, even after crises like Boipatong and, even more serious, the assassination by right-wingers of the hugely popular Chris Hani on 10 April 1993.

The Record of Understanding signified the resumption of formal multi-party negotiations, even though it was not until 1 April 1993 that the Multi-Party Negotiating Process (MPNP) started. Concessions were made by both sides: the government confirmed the ANC's demand that an elected constitution-making body draft and adopt a new (and final) constitution, while the ANC confirmed the government's demand that the constitution-making body be bound by 'agreed constitutional principles' that would emerge from the MPNP. Moreover, the ANC accepted the government's insistence that constitutional continuity be ensured by requiring the elected constitution-making body to act also as an interim parliament. Of crucial importance was the agreement that an interim 'government of national unity' should function within an interim constitution which would provide for national and regional government during the transition.

Herein lay the nucleus of the constitutional deal that was the basis of progress in the negotiations during 1993. It was complemented by a significant development in the ANC whereby it agreed, on 18 November 1992, that a Government of National Unity would be required even after the adoption of a new constitution. The initiative for this strategic repositioning came from Joe Slovo of the South African Communist Party and one of the ANC's leading theoreticians. His recommendations were embodied in a document entitled 'Negotiations: A Strategic Perspective', which was adopted on 18 November by the ANC's National Working Committee. The document analyses the stages in the conflict, noting that while the 'apartheid power bloc' had been weakened, 'the liberation movement did not have the immediate capacity to overthrow the regime': a 'balance of forces' existed, and although the ANC had made important gains and was sure that it commanded majority support, it suffered persistent weaknesses of capacity while 'the regime' could 'endlessly delay while consolidating its hold on power and restructuring in order to undermine future democratic transformation'.

The document accepted that the balance of forces and the interests of the country would require a government of national unity, with the proviso that the parties which had lost the election would not be able to paralyse the government. In line with this appraisal, the document acknowledged the 'vast potential to destabilise a fledgling democracy' of the army, police and civil service. While a restructuring of these institutions was necessary, it was also necessary in the meantime to address the question of job security, retrenchment packages and a general amnesty as part of a negotiated settlement. In short, wholesale dismissals of white state employees were not plausible.

The preceding paragraphs show how the negotiating process was pact-driven. As the major actors, the ANC and the NP government have been able to ensure that if they reach agreement the process can go forward. The cost of this *modus operandi*, however, has been the alienation of Chief Mangosuthu Buthelezi and the Inkatha Freedom Party from the MPNP. Buthelezi, who has developed a hatred of the ANC, was incensed by the Record of Understanding's implicit assumption of ANC/ government hegemony, even over issues of critical interest to Inkatha, such as the position of hostel dwellers and the carrying of traditional weapons. His reaction derived in part from pique at no longer being regarded as one of the 'big three' leaders. None of de Klerk's reassurances that no slight had been intended assuaged his anger. Moreover, Buthelezi was opposed to the principle that an elected constitution-making body should draft the final constitution. His stand on this issue had been made clear at CODESA, and he was in no mood to compromise. Buthelezi's fiefdom was KwaZulu, where the IFP held unchallenged sway, with the assistance of the KwaZulu police force, whose partisan behaviour led many opponents to regard it as little more than Inkatha's private army.

The formal Multi-Party Negotiating Process was reconstituted with additional participants in the form of the Pan Africanist Congress, the KwaZulu government, the Conservative Party, the Afrikaner Volksunie or AVU (a more moderate right-wing party that had broken away from the CP), and traditional leaders from the Transvaal, Orange Free State and Cape. If the organizations present at CODESA represented over 80 per cent of the future electorate, those participating in the MPNP increased the figure to virtually 100 per cent.

The wider spread of representation at the MPNP meant that consensus would be more difficult to obtain. At CODESA 'sufficient consensus' was taken to mean that consensus was 'sufficient' when there were enough organizations in agreement to enable the process to go forward. The MPNP tried to tighten the definition and to create mechanisms whereby non-consenting organizations could appeal against decisions, but essentially the concept meant exactly what it had meant at CODESA;

in turn, this meant that if the ANC (and its allies) and the NP and the government (they were represented by separate delegations) were in agreement, 'sufficient consensus' was almost certain to be reached. The obvious problem was that the same organizations were regular dissenters and could claim to be steamrollered. The regular dissenters were Inkatha, the CP, the AVU, and the governments of Bophuthatswana and Ciskei*, which formed the core of the Concerned South Africans Group (COSAG). COSAG thereafter transformed itself into the Freedom Alliance, which is discussed below.

The MPNP faced two tasks: to draft an interim constitution, including Constitutional Principles that would bind a future constitution-making body, and to 'level the playing-fields' for a future election. Under intense pressure from its impatient constituency, the ANC demanded that an election date be set. On 3 July 1993 the Council of the MPNP agreed to 27 April 1994. Inkatha and the CP walked out in protest.

Fixing the election date was risky since it would be extremely difficult thereafter to postpone it. Clearly, it will be no ordinary election since millions of new voters will regard it not only as a vote for the party of their choice but also as an act of affirmation of their new-found equal citizenship. The election will be an emotional catharsis, an *uhuru*† election with a vengeance.

Determining the date had contradictory effects on the MPNP. It imparted a sense of urgency to the proceedings and thus forced the negotiators to adhere to deadlines; but it also imposed enormous strain on participants. Since the draft interim constitution had to be enacted into law by parliament, during a short specially convened session commencing on 22 November, the final debates were conducted with unseemly haste. The almost complete draft constitution was finally agreed to by twenty-one organizations on 17 November and was thereafter completed and rushed to parliament.

The election on 27 April 1994 and the constitution in terms of which it will be held will shape the context of politics for some time to come. Accordingly, it is necessary to summarize the provisions of the constitution and ancillary legislation before examining the configuration of political forces and possible outcomes of the election.

---

*Two of the four so-called independent homelands, or TBVC states, the other two being Transkei and Venda.

†*Uhuru* is the Swahili word for 'freedom', widely used in Africa to refer to the exuberant sense of liberation attendant upon independence.

Interim arrangements

As has been noted, an important part of the MPNP's work was devoted to 'levelling the playing-fields' – characteristic South African parlance for ensuring that the governing NP derived no electoral benefit from its incumbency. The linchpin of the various mechanisms is the *Transitional Executive Council* (TEC), which was given statutory form by parliament and came into operation in December 1993. The objects of the TEC are to create a climate for free political participation by eliminating impediments to legitimate political activity and intimidation and ensuring that no government or administration (which includes the South African government and 'homeland' administrations) 'exercises any of its powers in such a way as to advantage or prejudice any political party'.

Each participant in the MPNP is entitled to representation by one member on the Council. Much of the work of the TEC will be performed by seven multi-party sub-councils that will operate under its control. The sub-councils cover: (1) regional and local government and traditional authorities; (2) law and order, stability and security; (3) defence; (4) finance; (5) foreign affairs; (6) status of women; and (7) intelligence. The TEC is empowered to obtain information regarding any proposed decision or action by a government, administration or political party that is 'likely to have a bearing on the objects of the Council'. If the Council or a sub-council believes that any decision or action is likely to have an adverse effect on a fair and free election, it may, after hearing representations, order that the decision or action not be proceeded with.

Although government spokesmen have insisted that the TEC is neither a 'super-cabinet' nor a parallel government, its advisory, monitoring and veto powers are likely to make it a watchdog with teeth. It is highly probable that as tensions mount in the run-up to the election there will be considerable friction within the TEC. In principle the TEC is to apply also to the 'independent' homelands, including Bophuthatswana and Ciskei, as well as to KwaZulu, all of which have declined to participate.* Similar refusals to cooperate can be anticipated from (white) local authorities controlled by the CP.

Complementing the TEC are other mechanisms. Of these the *Independent Electoral Commission* deserves mention. It is to be an impartial body, with an elaborate mechanism for hearing and adjudicating upon complaints. At its apex is the Special Electoral Court, presided over by a judge of the Appellate Division of the Supreme Court. The Court will

---

*The Ciskei government agreed in early January 1994 to participate in the TEC.

serve also as a final court of appeal for disputes that arise in the TEC. Ultimately, the task of the Independent Electoral Commission will be to pronounce the elections 'free and fair'.

No democratizing state has rivalled South Africa in the complex bureaucracy it has assembled to ensure free and fair elections. Undoubtedly this reflects the intense suspicion of the NP government by its opponents. Indirectly it also reflects the absence of a widely shared democratic political culture and the consequent view that institutions of the kind discussed above are necessary to force people and parties to behave democratically. On paper the institutions appear to provide foolproof safeguards, but they have yet to be tested against the stubborn reality of intolerance and profoundly undemocratic attitudes that underly the supposedly democratic stance that many organizations profess.

The interim constitution

The interim constitution is classically liberal-democratic in form. Its major features are: a bicameral parliamentary system based upon the principle of the sovereignty of the constitution; a justiciable bill of rights; an independent judiciary, including a constitutional court; an electoral system based upon proportional representation; and hybrid federal/unitary arrangements.

Government of National Unity

The core of the constitution is the provision for a Government of National Unity (GNU), which had been agreed to in broad outline by the ANC and the NP government in 1992. The section on the executive provides for a President who is to be elected by the National Assembly. The President has to be a member of the National Assembly, but once chosen as President he/she must vacate the Assembly seat. The President is to function as head of state and convenor of the cabinet. Every party holding at least 80 seats out of the 400 in the National Assembly may designate an Executive Deputy President from among the members of the National Assembly. Should no party or only one party hold 80 seats, the parties holding the largest and second largest numbers can designate Executive Deputy Presidents.

The cabinet is to consist of the President, the deputies and not more than 27 ministers appointed by the President. Each party holding at least 20 seats in the National Assembly shall be entitled to a proportionate number of ministerial portfolios relative to the number of seats held by other parties. The President is to appoint ministers to the portfolios allocated to the qualifying parties after consultation with his/her deputies and the leaders of the eligible parties. The President can dismiss a minister if requested to do so by the leader of the party which designated the minister.

The most recent draft of the constitution has done away with the (probably unworkable) attempt to stipulate required cabinet majorities for particular votes. All that is required now is that the cabinet seek consensus in accordance with the spirit underlying the Government of National Unity and the need for effective government. This is the standard procedure in cabinets in virtually all parliamentary systems: votes are not taken. How it will work in the circumstances of a compulsory coalition is likely to be problematic. Since the cabinet will be the core of the power-sharing arrangement for five years, a challenge will be posed to the good sense and cooperativeness of the leaders of the parties represented. Since twenty seats represent 5 per cent of the vote, one can anticipate, on the basis of recent polls, that the ANC, NP, IFP and CP will all obtain some cabinet representation. Consensus will not be easily forthcoming.

Votes of no confidence in the cabinet are possible, whereupon the President is obliged to dissolve parliament and call a general election, or reconstitute the cabinet.

Provincial government

The second major feature of the constitution is its provision for provincial government. Almost certainly these provisions will change, as will the provincial boundaries recommended by the Regional Boundary Demarcation Commission. The argument has focused primarily on whether the system should be federal, unitary or 'hybrid'. Initially, the ANC conceded that some not very significant powers (most of which, in any case, were local authority functions) could be vested exclusively in the provinces but the central government would retain extensive powers of override. An act of the (central) parliament will prevail over provincial law if the latter

(a) deals with a matter that cannot be regulated effectively by provincial legislation;
(b) deals with a matter that, to be performed effectively, requires to be regulated or coordinated by uniform norms or standards that apply countrywide;
(c) materially prejudices the economic, health or security interests of another province or the country as a whole.

Furthermore, national legislation will prevail if it is necessary to set minimum standards countrywide for the rendering of public services or when it is necessary for the determination of national economic policies, the maintenance of economic unity, the protection of the environment, the promotion of inter-provincial commerce, the protection of the common market in respect of mobility of goods, services, capital or labour, or the maintenance of national security. An indirect protection of provincial powers is provided in another clause: an act of parliament shall prevail over a provincial law, as in the circumstances set out above, only if it applies uniformly across the Republic.

These are sweeping powers of override that cast strong doubt on the federal character of the constitution. Moreover, later drafts of the constitution make no reference to exclusive provincial powers but, instead, expand the list of concurrent powers that may be exercised jointly by the central and provincial governments. These include very important issues like education (except at the tertiary level), health, housing, local government, language policy, police (with certain limitations) and welfare services.

The clauses dealing with provincial finance and fiscal affairs entitle provinces to an equitable share of revenue collected nationally, but provincial taxing powers are limited by the requirement of parliament's authorization. Provision is made for a Financial and Fiscal Commission which will advise, oversee and make recommendations regarding the financial and fiscal requirements of national, provincial and local governments. Although the Commission has only advisory powers, it is likely to be a crucially important institution.

The draft constitution must be considered as defining a basically unitary state with some federal fig-leaves. Political systems may evolve in more federal or more unitary directions, and what is crucial in determining these directions is the extent of mobilization at the regional level. Belgium and Spain are examples of unitary states that have shifted in a federal direction as a result of regional pressure.

Another provision in the draft has distinct implications for this issue: the contentious decision (opposed by the DP, PAC and Freedom Alliance) that the voter shall cast one vote for a party list that will determine representation at both the central and the provincial level. Apart from being profoundly undemocratic, this will be sure to have strong indirect centralizing effects by penalizing parties that have only provincial bases. The ostensible reason, advanced by the ANC, is that having to cast two votes will confuse illiterate and unsophisticated voters. While there is undeniably truth in this, the real reason is the ANC's fear that voters might (as they have done in some mock, experimental ballots) vote, respectively, for their first and second choices of party, e.g. vote 1 goes to the ANC, but vote 2 goes to the PAC or the IFP.

The Constitutional Court

Another innovation is the Constitutional Court, whose ten members are to be appointed on the recommendation of the Judicial Service Commission, which will also appoint Supreme Court judges. The Judicial Service Commission will be presided over by the Chief Justice; it will be composed of representatives from a wide range of legal bodies and four Senators designated *en bloc* by the Senate by a two-thirds majority.

The Constitutional Court will have wide powers: it is the court of final instance over all matters relating to the interpretation, protection and enforcement of all provisions of the constitution, including the violation of rights, the constitutionality of executive conduct, laws, and disputes of a constitutional nature between organs of the state at all levels. In other words, it will probably have a major role to play in interpreting the wide terms of the federal provisions. Judicial review will become an important feature of the South African constitution; legislation and executive actions will be tested against the bill of rights, which includes clauses permitting affirmative action and the restitution of land claimed by dispossessed people.

The draft constitution is specific on the circumstances under which states of emergency can be declared and how the suspension of liberties will be qualified. The essence of the provision is that the courts may be required to validate the executive's decision, if it is challenged, and they will continue to act as a watchdog over citizens' rights. The principle of *habeas corpus* is restored, and security legislation is brought into line with comparable legislation in other liberal democracies. Indeed, the courts are required in interpreting this section to 'promote the values which underlie an open and democratic society based on freedom and equality'.

No constitution is entirely resistant to the machinations of power-hungry politicians, but it can be said of the draft constitution that its provisions which aim at the prevention of abuse of power are tough.

The Constitutional Assembly

Another section deals with the constitution-making function of parliament *qua* Constitutional Assembly. The Constitutional Assembly is to be bound by 33 Constitutional Principles that are listed in a schedule, most of which are already embodied in the draft interim constitution. The Constitutional Court will have to certify that the final constitution complies with the Constitutional Principles; this reflects the compromise between the ANC's demand for an all-powerful Constituent Assembly and the government's refusal to yield untrammelled power to an elected body.

The draft of the final constitution's text is to be adopted within two years of the commencement of the new parliament by a two-thirds majority vote of the Constitutional Assembly. A deadlock-breaking mechanism is included: if the Constitutional Assembly cannot muster the required two-thirds vote, the draft is to be referred to a panel of five constitutional experts, none of whom may hold office in a political party. The panel is to be selected by a two-thirds majority of the Constitutional Assembly. If the draft is amended on the unanimous advice of the panel and still cannot gain the required two-thirds majority, but is supported by a simple majority, the President can submit the draft to a referendum that will require a 60 per cent acceptance. If the draft is not accepted by the electorate or if a new text is not adopted within two years, parliament will be dissolved and an election held. The Constitutional Assembly thus elected is required to approve a new text within one year by a majority of 60 per cent of all the members.

This is an elaborate procedure. The interesting question is whether the final draft is likely to differ from the interim constitution, given the binding nature of the scheduled Constitutional Principles. Government spokespersons say they will be similar; ANC sources decline to comment. Radical changes are unlikely, but much depends on the size of the ANC's majority in the 1994 election. If it and its allies win over 66.6 per cent of the vote, which is a distinct possibility, there may be pressure for changes. Only the Constitutional Court will stand between the agreed Principles and the ANC's possible wish to drive through its own preferred (and more centralist) constitution. Who serves on the court thus becomes a critically important issue.

Summary

In summary, the draft interim constitution is a messy and inconclusive document, the result of inevitable compromises – and the continuing efforts to retain sufficient flexibility to draw the Freedom Alliance (or parts of it) back into the process. Apart from ensuring continuity, the draft constitution may possess the advantage of placing restraints upon the contest for power. Adam Przeworski has written: 'Constitutions that are observed and last for a long time are those that reduce the stakes of political battles. Pretenders to office can expect to reach it; losers can expect to come back.'[7] The GNU, the supposedly federal features, the protection accorded to private property and the job security promised to white employees of the state have enabled de Klerk to claim that all of the undertakings he gave to white voters during the referendum in 1992 have been honoured. The compromise represented by the constitution, however, is a considerable derogation from the NP's original constitutional proposals of 1991: for example, power-sharing (a term the ANC declines to use) will last for only five years, and the quasi-federalism of the constitution is hardly tantamount to the original proposal for the maximum devolution of power to regional and local governments.

Constitutions, moreover, resemble 'parchment barriers' (to borrow Madison's phrase[8]). South Africa, like virtually every other African state, has not proved hospitable to constitutionalism. It lacks a democratic political culture. Indeed, perhaps the most notable feature of its political culture is a tendency to view politics as a zero-sum game, in which capture of the state is the supreme prize. Such a predisposition is inimical to the continual need for delicate compromises that will be required if the GNU is to operate successfully.

Party prospects

The African National Congress

One may question whether the ANC, in view of its history as a liberation movement, is likely to be able successfully to transform itself into a political party capable of observing the restraints and respect for constitutional rules that liberal democracy presupposes. There are several dimensions to this issue. First, there is the character of the ANC and its constituency. Since its inception in 1912 the ANC has essentially been a coalition (a 'broad church', in Mandela's phrase) of ideologically diverse elements unified by a common opposition to segregation and apartheid. Its supporters include all shades of opinion, from liberals to hardline Stalinists; it declines to call itself a 'socialist' movement, but there can be little doubt that much of the ANC's theoretical and strategic discourse has been conducted in a Marxist paradigm.

Close cooperation with the South African Communist Party (SACP) shaped the terms of the ANC's discourse in significant ways. Apart from their major role as a conduit for funding from Soviet and other Eastern bloc sources, the Communists provided organizational skills as well as the services of many dedicated individuals who formed the backbone of the ANC's armed wing, Umkhonto we Sizwe. The demise of Marxism-Leninism and the accommodation the ANC has been required to make with the white political and business establishments have opened up the internal debate and enabled it to accept more pragmatic economic policy options than originally seemed likely.

The long years of exile in Lusaka suffered by many ANC leaders had, at least, the salutary effect of exposing them to the consequences of economic mismanagement and corruption. Zambia's former one-party system and the political sclerosis it induced also innoculated the ANC against any thoughts of adopting a similar system in South Africa.

The problems caused by ideological diffuseness remain, however, and are likely to deepen rather than decrease. As an interclass organization, the ANC is bound to feel increasing tension as intra-African class differences widen. On the one hand, it has a close alliance with the Congress of South African Trade Unions (COSATU); on the other, the National African Chamber of Commerce (NAFCOC) also tends to be ANC-aligned. As the African bourgeoisie grows, accompanied by the rapid growth of a bureaucratic bourgeois class, sharper conflicts of interest may be anticipated within the 'broad church'. Complicating these possible developments is the huge number of unemployed (discussed in Chapter 4), many of whom will support the ANC. COSATU, for all its pretensions to the contrary, undeniably represents an 'aristocracy of labour'. Indeed, there can be little doubt that its wage demands have cost thousands of jobs and contributed to the inflationary spiral.

Elsewhere in black Africa the relationship between governing parties and the trade union movement has commonly been a fraught one, with their interests diverging after independence. Although COSATU is a member of the ANC alliance and twenty COSATU members will be included on the ANC's electoral list, this is no guarantee of durable cooperation.

With the removal of the ANC's historical *raison d'être*, opposition to segregation and apartheid, a powerful source of cohesion is removed. For the time being, the ANC's status as the premier liberation movement and the towering stature of Mandela will enable it to ride increasing tensions within its support base. Patronage may be a handy substitute source of cohesion, but its supply will be limited and its selective distribution could exacerbate tensions.

Another problem the ANC has had to cope with in its transition from banned movement to political organization is integrating returning exiles, released political prisoners and demobilized Umkhonto we Sizwe guerrillas with an internal leadership that had emerged in the United Democratic Front, the unions and the Mass Democratic Movement in the 1980s.* As has been the case in Namibia, tensions were immediately evident.

Further tensions were caused by a clash of leadership styles: inevitably, exile forced upon the ANC a 'top-down' style that was no doubt exacerbated by the 'vanguardism' of SACP members in key positions; in contrast, the constituent organizations of the Mass Democratic Movement and the unions prided themselves on their internally democratic processes. Even Mandela was subjected to criticism for the leadership's allegedly high-handed style. At the ANC's national conference in July 1991 he acknowledged criticism of the way in which the leadership had handled the negotiations thus far:

> One of the criticisms has been that there has not been sufficient consultation before we entered negotiations on a particular issue. There has also been the fair criticism that there has been no systematic and regular reporting on the outcome of negotiations, and that the membership has remained ignorant of what was going on in these discussions. We fully acknowledge that criticism.[9]

As yet the ANC has declined to describe itself as a party, preferring to retain the term 'national liberation movement'. A resolution adopted at the 1991 conference read:

> That the ANC is a national liberation movement providing leadership to its members and the oppressed and democratic forces of South Africa generally, over a wide range of issues. The ANC is not a political party. In formulating our policies for a democratic South Africa these should relate to mass struggles and provide opportunities for the masses to assert their just demands.[10]

The resolution reflected the prevailing view that a party was too limited a vehicle to accommodate the ANC's vision of itself as a 'broad church' that acted in the name of 'the people' and not merely in the narrow interest of a political organization. Becoming a party would require a

---

*The United Democratic Front was formed in 1983 to protest against the tricameral constitution. It was subsequently subsumed under the umbrella of the even more diffuse Mass Democratic Movement.

greater preciseness in policies instead of the fuzzy 'all-things-to-all-persons' approach to policy-making that has hitherto characterized the ANC. Strengthening this view was the practical consideration that many foreign governments and non-governmental organizations (NGOs) could fund liberation movements but were not permitted to fund parties.

There are inherent dangers to democracy in this Jacobin view of 'the people'. As Marina Ottaway has argued, the transformation from liberation movement to political party is a difficult process that has not been accomplished successfully in any African state:

> What characterised liberation movements ... was the stress on unity, the rejection of partisan divisions as destructive of the new nation, and the illusion that an entire country could have a single purpose and accept a single representative to speak as the 'mouthpiece of an oppressed nation'. Political parties operating in a democratic framework, on the other hand, do not pretend to represent a people or a nation, but specific constituencies.[11]

Many in the ANC espouse a notion of 'revolutionary legitimacy', which manifests itself in a tendency to regard only those who participated in 'the struggle' – domestically or abroad – as having credibility or legitimacy. Those, like Chief Mangosuthu Buthelezi and the IFP, who sought to use apartheid institutions against the apartheid system, are execrated as 'collaborators', 'puppets' or 'agents of the state'. Overcoming the stigma of 'collaboration' requires absolute repudiation of the system and alignment with the ANC.

The factors discussed in the preceding paragraphs consolidate the ANC's view of its entitlement to be the beneficiary of the 'transfer of power to the people'. Its self-image is that of 'a government-in-waiting'. Although Mandela has frequently said that he wants no more than 'an ordinary democracy', and although the ANC stresses its commitment to the development of a strong civil society and the pluralism that makes it possible, many critics remain sceptical of the ANC's genuineness, and accuse it of hegemonic aspirations. They point to its strong influence over sporting bodies like the National Olympic Committee of South Africa (NOCSA), cultural organizations, religion (as in the South African Council of Churches), certain universities, and a wide range of NGOs which, allegedly, act as sources of patronage for the ANC. Fears have been expressed that the new board of the South African Broadcasting Corporation, appointed in 1993, has a majority of members, including the chairperson, who are broadly sympathetic to the ANC and may, over time, slant the electronic media in its favour.

Other criticisms focus upon the intolerance of many grass-roots ANC supporters, who have prevented opposition organizations from holding meetings. Such behaviour has been condemned by the leadership, but the message has not filtered down. This is hardly surprising. The poverty, squalor and violence of many African townships do not create environments conducive to democratic practices. The breakdown of family and school control, in particular, and the sheer frustration caused by endemic unemployment create resistance to all forms of authority. 'Making the townships ungovernable' was an ANC-inspired strategy that succeeded all too well: the ANC will have to cope with the genie that was released from the bottle.

The forthcoming election poses a major challenge to the ANC. That it will emerge as the biggest single organization is a foregone conclusion. The only doubt is whether it will win a two-thirds majority; polls published in November 1993 showed it enjoying 64 per cent of the total vote, so this majority is well within its reach.[12]

As the dominant partner in the GNU, the ANC will face a daunting challenge: major responsibility for ruling a divided and turbulent society that will for a long time bear the scars of its history. The ANC will be confronted with immediate demands from its constituency and the consequent temptation to engage in free-spending populist policies that will have disastrous economic consequences. Thus far in the campaign, its leaders, while advocating far-reaching reconstruction measures, have warned their followers not to expect instant gratification of their material aspirations. As Thabo Mbeki, chairman of the ANC (and a strong contender for Mandela's post when he retires), puts it: 'There is a growing realisation of constraints on policy and desires. We have to address the issues around deprivation, but I would like to make it very clear that you cannot have liberation on Monday and a house on Tuesday.'[13] The ANC will be incapable of immediately redressing the (legitimate) grievances of its supporters. Political skill of a high order will be required if inflated election promises are to be avoided without destroying any (credible) hope that conditions will incrementally improve.

The National Party

During 1990 de Klerk and some of his colleagues made bold to claim that a revitalized NP, which had abolished apartheid, opened its membership to all races and committed itself to democracy, could actually defeat the

ANC in an election. By mid-1993 the picture was different: polls were showing a steady decline in support for the NP among all races; by November 1993 a Human Sciences Research Council (HSRC) poll tentatively estimated NP support to be a mere 15 to 18 per cent. Among whites the party's support had declined from approximately 50 per cent in February to less than one-third; among Africans the small support (8 per cent) recorded earlier had dropped to virtually zero.[14]

NP officials acknowledged the decline, but claimed that the polls understated the extent of support and insisted that the target of 40 per cent of the vote was attainable. Olaus van Zyl, the NP's Manager of National Information, claimed that much of the eroded support was capable of being regained since it had not gone to other parties.[15] This view is partly confirmed by the HSRC poll quoted above, with the proviso that notwithstanding some recouping the NP is unlikely to win more than about 20 per cent of the vote.

Why has this decline occurred? There are several causes. The failure of the NP to gain much African support and, possibly, less Coloured and Indian support than it hoped for reflects its inability to shake off its image as 'the party of apartheid'. The converse is the perception among apprehensive, insecure whites that the NP has 'capitulated' to ANC demands. The party that once afforded them power, protection and patronage can no longer deliver. Sustained attacks by Mandela on de Klerk's integrity and continual accusations from both left and right that the NP government is a 'lame duck' have exacted their toll. A leaked internal NP document quotes Dr Dawie de Villiers, Minister for Public Enterprises and the NP's chief negotiator in the MPNP, as saying: 'We have one problem. People believe that the ANC is already governing the country and that its permission is necessary for all decisions in respect of sport, culture, etc. This must be denied.'[16] Denials, however, would not be altogether convincing since the ANC has, in fact, amply demonstrated that its capacity to orchestrate 'mass action' with seriously disruptive consequences gives it an effective veto power. The installation of the TEC in December 1993 merely gives this political reality statutory form.

De Klerk and his party have also been seriously damaged by continuing revelations of scandals, including large-scale corruption in homeland administrations, corrupt deals supposedly aimed at circumventing sanctions, 'dirty tricks' and the assassination of opponents carried out by agents of the state in the name of resisting the 'total onslaught'.[17] The latter doctrine, devised by a paranoid security establishment in the 1980s, became a pretext for numerous authoritarian and murderous activities.

The problem for de Klerk was that information about what had happened dribbled out only after his accession to the Presidency. He, nevertheless, has had to incur the odium that resulted. His (genuine) efforts to stop the excesses of various 'dirty tricks' operatives may have been substantially successful – the point is debatable – but vicious, internecine political violence has continued. Mandela's repeated allegations of de Klerk's complicity miss the point that de Klerk has been more seriously damaged by the violence than any other leader, with the exception of Buthelezi. Coupled with political violence has been sharply increasing criminal violence, including numerous cases of the brutal slaying of elderly whites on isolated farms. This, too, has rubbed off on de Klerk by strengthening the perception that his administration has been unable to protect communities and has 'lost control'.

As the correspondence columns of Afrikaans newspapers show, many traditional NP supporters have the gravest misgivings about where the transition will lead. It reflects a changed situation, from one in which the NP government's power was unchallenged to one in which its capacity to rule effectively has been seriously impaired. In the circumstances, the transformation initiated by de Klerk must be acknowledged as one of the more remarkable feats of political leadership in the twentieth century. Faced with severe attacks from both left and right he has stood his ground, not once wavering in his determination to secure a settlement. This has required skill and courage. Hardly less remarkable has been his ability to keep his caucus substantially intact, in spite of regular murmurings from apprehensive backbench MPs and well-attested reports of divisions within the cabinet. The backbenchers reflect, in turn, the fears of the grass-roots party members, to say nothing of their own nervousness at the imminent prospect of losing their seats.

Unlike his predecessor, de Klerk has managed to combine firm leadership with a capacity to listen attentively. The seven 'antis' (as they have been called) in the cabinet do not represent a unified bloc of hawks: they vary in view from those who are deeply unhappy with the negotiations and allege that too much has been conceded to the ANC, to those who have reservations about particular aspects of the emergent constitutional settlement. Personality differences are also said to be a factor.[18] A significant cause of the differences is the question as to whether the NP should, in the interests of creating the strongest possible anti-ANC bloc, form alliances with parties such as the IFP, other small homeland parties, and elements of the right wing.

Relations with the IFP have deteriorated badly, to the dismay of those

Nationalists, especially in Natal, who regard it as a strong bulwark against the ANC. Others, however, note the decline in the IFP's support among Africans and argue that an alliance with Buthelezi would be fatal to the NP's efforts to win African votes. Whatever their misgivings and poor morale, Nationalist backbenchers, like some 40 per cent of CP supporters, do not believe that the CP proposals for 'self-determination' are viable.

During its provincial congresses in September and October 1993, the NP officially accepted the necessity of alliances or cooperation with parties which shared its basic principles and values. Specifically excluded were 'racist elements' in the Afrikaner-Volksfront, an umbrella body linking right-wing parties.[19] No indications have yet emerged of possible alliance partners. They will probably be limited to minor homeland parties which, in any case, are likely to be eliminated in the election.

In large part de Klerk owed his resounding victory in the 1992 referendum to the guarantees in the constitutional proposals for which he sought a mandate. When faced with a choice between confrontation and negotiation most whites opted for the latter, with the expectation that guarantees would somehow secure their position. These included permanent power-sharing in a federal system in which power was devolved to the maximum possible extent to regions; a free market economy; and guarantees for the status of Afrikaans. The extent to which the interim constitution embodies these guarantees has become a major issue in view of allegations that the NP 'capitulated' to the ANC in the concluding sessions of the MPNP. It was naive to suppose that the NP could have secured a constitutional blueprint that contained all of its proposals in virtually unchanged form. Compromises had to be made, but growing recognition throughout 1993 of the ANC's formidable strength in the prospective electorate tipped the scales somewhat in its favour in the negotiations.

Permanent power-sharing with a collective presidency was not only unsaleable but, most probably, unworkable. Senior NP negotiators realized this, and acknowledged that it would weaken the opposition by locking the principal parties into a forced union. It could be more important for the ANC's major opponent to remain in opposition 'instead of accepting co-responsibility for the actions of a future government'. Moreover, power-sharing could be achieved in various ways, one of which was strong regional government.[20]

The compromise, a coalition GNU for five years, is probably the best deal the NP could have made in the circumstances, but it is unlikely to allay suspicions of 'capitulation'. Similarly, the putatively federal provisions of the constitution offer, at best, some federal potential, but it remains difficult to see how this can be realized if the ANC, like most governments in Africa, sets itself on a strongly centralist course. Hopes expressed by federalists in South Africa in 1909 that the Union constitution could be pushed in an increasingly federalist direction were not realized. History could repeat itself.

As far as language is concerned, the retention of Afrikaans as an official language has allayed some fears, as well as enabling the NP government to honour an important commitment. How having no fewer than eleven official languages will work in practice is problematic. Many Afrikaners fear, with good reason, that the status of Afrikaans will inevitably decline as English increasingly becomes 'the language of record'.

The Freedom Alliance

By December 1993 the institutions created to carry the transition forward had not yet become 'the only game in town', to quote Przeworski's phrase. The organizations and governments forming the Freedom Alliance were resisting participation in the TEC and it remained unclear whether they would participate in the April election. The major right-wing organization, the CP, demanded a *volkstaat* in which Afrikaners could enjoy self-determination; Bophuthatswana and Ciskei, nominally independent states, maintained that their sovereign status required that reincorporation into South Africa (provided for by legislation agreed to by the MPNP) would first have to be approved by their respective governing bodies; Inkatha and the KwaZulu government remained staunchly opposed to the principle of a Constitutional Assembly drafting the final constitution, and demanded a highly decentralized federal system, in fact one verging on confederation.

At the time of writing it was not possible to predict what would happen, since bilateral talks between the Freedom Alliance and, respectively, the government and the ANC were continuing. On 15 November the FA issued a statement containing its 'final positions' on critical issues: it demanded that exclusive regional powers (without specifying which) should be entrenched in the constitution; that provision be made for 'asymmetry', i.e. 'that regions be allowed varying degrees of powers at different times, as they evolve and mature; that regions be permitted to levy their own taxes and raise additional funds autonomously; that regions be permitted to adopt and amend their own constitutions within the framework of the bill of rights and the main provisions of the national constitution; and that the mode of appointing judges to the Constitutional Court be altered to obviate the possibility of political manipulation'.[21]

None of these demands is incapable of a compromise resolution, and two of them, those relating to provincial constitution-making and appointments of Constitutional Court judges, have already been met. Strangely, the FA statement, said by its chairman to have been unanimous, makes no reference to the CP's demand for a race-based *volkstaat* in a confederal relationship with the rest of South Africa – a demand repeated by the CP subsequent to 15 November! No doubt the discrepancy is attributable to the appreciable differences among the various components of the FA and within individual components themselves. There are clearly pragmatists, moderates and hardliners within the AVF, while several of Buthelezi's key lieutenants are reported to be deeply concerned about his intractability. Rowan Cronje, chief negotiator for the Bophuthatswana government and chairman of the FA, is also reported as eager to reach a settlement.[22]

The question is, what leverage or spoiling capacity do the FA and its respective components possess: is it sufficient to sabotage the transition, and, even worse, to plunge South Africa into civil war? The HSRC polls, cited above, indicate that the FA is supported by 14–18 per cent of the electorate (putting it neck-and-neck with the NP); if that figure is disaggregated the IFP is said to have 10 per cent, the CP 3–8 per cent, and other right-wing groups one per cent.[23] A Markinor poll of 800 whites during November 1993 found that only 28 per cent favoured the creation of a white homeland; only 22 per cent believed it was feasible; and only 14 per cent of the sample, including slightly more than 40 per cent of CP and AVF supporters, said that they would be willing to move to it.[24]

It was evident during the 1992 referendum that many CP supporters ignored their party's call to vote against continuation of the negotiating process. The NP is banking upon a similar switch of allegiance in the 1994 election on the assumption that many conservative whites will want to support a party that appears to offer the most effective counterweight to the ANC.

Bellicose talk, threats of civil disobedience and strike action that could paralyse mines and power stations (where many right-wingers work) have been frequent. Conservatives declared that the installation of the TEC would be tantamount to a 'declaration of war'. Evidence exists of substantial arms caches, supplies of explosives and other preparations for counter-revolution. Periodic episodes of right-wing violence have

43

occurred, and there will be more in the run-up to the election. An imminent possibility is the declaration by the CP of an internal 'unilateral declaration of independence' of a demarcated *volkstaat* and the creation of 'parallel structures'. The CP controls 65 (white) local authorities in the Transvaal rural areas and six in the Orange Free State. It claims that it is testing white opinion to ascertain interest in joining a putative *volkstaat*.

The viability of such a breakaway *volkstaat*, which would in any case have a large African population, would be minimal, since it would be unrecognized, landlocked and inextricably dependent on the rest of South Africa in myriad ways. Neither the ANC nor the NP could tolerate a *volkstaat* in which Africans were relegated to inferior citizenship status. Much the same analysis holds good for the recalcitrant homelands, whether independent or not. Ciskei and KwaZulu, for example, derive over 75 per cent of their revenues from the South African government; Bophuthatswana, which is better-endowed, is in a more favourable situation but is still not capable of surviving as a breakaway state. The majority of its population, as in Ciskei, is likely to support the ANC, with the result that any attempt to thwart reintegration would probably lead to large-scale uprisings.

The Inkatha Freedom Party

The case of KwaZulu is somewhat different since the IFP has strong support in the proposed Natal province; this tends, however, to be concentrated in the highly traditionalist areas in the north. The ANC is also strong in the province, and may even have an electoral edge on the IFP among African voters. The IFP has acquired some support among whites, including the defection of five white MPs (two Nationalists, two independent right-wingers and one Democrat), but its alliance with right-wingers has cost it some African support. It does not appear to have made much headway among the substantial Indian community. Predicting the electoral outcome in the province is made even more difficult by the high levels of violence, which cause many to keep their political affiliations secret. The violence also makes it difficult to foresee how unhindered campaigning can take place, since many areas are either IFP or ANC strongholds and therefore inaccessible to canvassers from the 'wrong' party. It is hard to see how this situation will change before the election.

The IFP is divided on the question of participation in the election. Buthelezi's intractability has caused tensions, and he has even incurred the displeasure of the Zulu King, Goodwill Zwelithini, normally considered to be a pliant ally of Buthelezi, for missing opportunities to reach an acceptable settlement.[25] While the debate continues and senior members voice contradictory views, the party's electoral machinery is nevertheless being oiled for action.

Conclusion

The loose ends in the transition process make predictions hazardous. It is, however, likely that the election will proceed on the scheduled date, even if circumstances in parts of the country are inimical to free campaigning. This is so because there is a widespread view that the consequences of postponing the election would be far more serious than the flaws in the electoral process. On this view the election is likely to be messy, violent and flawed, but not sufficiently so to obscure the picture of the electorate's choices.

Over 22 million people will be eligible to vote, of whom some 17 million will be Africans, voting for the first time in a democratic election. In the absence of electoral rolls, voters will vote at polling stations on production of an Identity Document. According to the Department of Home Affairs, 1.8 million voters, excluding those in the TBVC states, were still without IDs in November, although the Department was issuing 12,000 per day.[26] According to the Minister, 7,500 polling stations containing 22,500 polling booths and 14,900 ballot boxes will be required, with 135,000 officials in attendance.[27] Numerous local and foreign monitors will be present as well.

A high percentage poll should be anticipated, although serious levels of intimidation in areas of intense party conflict may offset this to some extent. To date, the most comprehensive survey of voter intentions is that carried out by an HSRC team which polled 8,366 Africans in non-metropolitan areas between March and May 1993.[28] They found that 77 per cent indicated an intention to vote, while 13 per cent said they would not. Only 54 per cent responded 'very sure' or 'sure' to a question as to whether they believed their vote would be secret. While most respondents could respond to probing questions about the various forms intimidation could take, only about 10 per cent acknowledged having been intimidated/ threatened, mocked/laughed at or attacked because of their political views.

Indications of a weakly developed democratic political culture were provided by the responses to two further questions: no fewer than 27 per cent approved or strongly approved of the breaking up of party meetings other than their own parties; 33 per cent disapproved or strongly disapproved, while 14 per cent neither approved nor disapproved and 25 per cent were uncertain. Only 41 per cent of respondents believed that there should be a parliamentary opposition, while 30 per cent believed there should not be, and a further 30 per cent were uncertain. The researchers observe that the argument of those opposed to the concept of an opposition derived from a belief that 'South Africa needed a strong, centralist government to ensure peace. Opposition to government merely caused conflict and violence.' The resemblance to arguments once invoked to justify one-party systems in Africa is striking.

The authors of the survey claim that the sample represented 79 per cent of all potential black voters in South Africa (including the TBVC states), and that some of the findings can be extrapolated to black voters generally. The avoidance of metropolitan areas no doubt means that many more sophisticated and knowledgeable respondents were excluded.

All parties are on record as agreeing to accept the outcome of the election if it is free and fair. Since the ANC is likely to win a commanding majority nationally, other parties are unlikely to be able to quarrel with the result; at the provincial level, however, several of the contests may be close-run. For example, in Natal, the IFP and the ANC will be involved in a major struggle, and neither may win an overall majority. While the principle of the GNU will apply also at the provincial level – each party winning at least 10 per cent of the seats in the provincial legislature will be entitled to a proportionate share of Executive Council portfolios – great importance will be attached to winning provincial majorities. The ANC is likely to win majorities in at least five of the nine provinces, but the outcome in four, Western Cape, Northern Cape, North-West and Natal, could be close.

It could be argued that a resounding ANC victory, nationally and provincially, would be the best guarantee of stability. Not only would convincing wins probably undercut haggles about how free and fair the elections were, but it might also give the ANC the sense of security that would enable it to behave generously to smaller parties, whose cooperation it will in any case need. The problem with this argument is that, while it may be true, it nevertheless tends to endorse what might be termed 'the Africa syndrome', where a single dominant party entrenches itself in power, becomes symbiotically related to the state, electorally impregnable, and, ultimately, politically sclerotic. Rotation of governing parties has not been a strong feature of African polities, and South Africa is unlikely to prove an exception. Better then, as a partial substitute, to have a political system in which minority parties can at least exercise power at the provincial level.

The minuscule level of white support for the ANC and African support for the NP shows the extent to which voting will be shaped by race. To some extent this will be mitigated by a fairly wide distribution of Coloured and Indian votes across the political spectrum. Racial polarity may also be reduced by the wish of all the parties (except the CP) to appeal to voters of all colours. Even so, voting will be largely ascriptive. 'Non-racialism' as an attitudinal predisposition will remain a utopian ideal for generations.

Constitutions should be judged by their ability to create structures that regulate and contain conflict within a democratic context. Durability is another important criterion, although it is likely to be determined by its success as a regulator. It must be stressed that the South African constitution is an interim one whose durability is, by definition, limited. Nevertheless it will shape constitutional thought and the context of politics, apart from the obligation of the Constitutional Assembly to incorporate the 33 Constitutional Principles in the final constitution. Moreover, if the interim constitution works satisfactorily this will make a persuasive case for persisting with its main provisions. The provisions for a GNU are of a temporary nature, but it is not impossible to imagine circumstances in which, aided and abetted by the list system of proportional representation, coalition government at both national and provincial levels became the norm. If the 'Africa syndrome' becomes reality (as it is in virtually all of Southern Africa where quasi-democratic systems have survived), it could be partly mitigated by a system of shifting coalitions that avoids another syndrome common in divided societies, that of the perpetually excluded minority.

Constitutions *per se* cannot secure the complete protection of minorities (however configured): bills of rights, proportional representation and other institutional mechanisms can facilitate their protection and perhaps ward off the worst effects of majority tyranny. The operation of the GNU may be decisive in shaping the pattern of majority/minority relations for far longer than the five-year period of its operation. Assuming (which one cannot) that the NP is the second-biggest party in the GNU, Mandela and de Klerk will face a serious test of leadership skills in their quest for a cooperative relationship that transcends their political differences. A period of stable, democratic government and a muting of the high levels of conflict is what South Africa needs.

No confident predictions can be made about whether the election will be conducive to peace. It may undercut the pretensions of those who have had recourse to violence; it may be a cathartic release, reminiscent of a boil being lanced. On the other hand, some right-wingers are likely to resort to violence, probably of a guerrilla nature. Buthelezi, too, will not accept defeat gracefully, but he has neither the support nor the resources of, say, Jonas Savimbi in Angola.

Constitutions are mere 'parchment barriers', but they are also symbolic statements of their drafters' aspirations. The strength of the interim constitution lies in the safeguards it erects against the abuse of power. They may not be insuperable, but their symbolism might teach South Africans a valuable lesson about the mistakes of their authoritarian past – and give them hope for a democratic future.

Notes

The author wishes to record his thanks for comments on an earlier draft to Ken Andrew, Leon Wessels and Virginia van der Vliet. None is to be blamed for errors of fact and the author alone is responsible for the opinions expressed.

1 Quoted in David Welsh, 'The outlook for a democratic South Africa', *International Affairs*, vol. 67, no. 4 (1991), p. 740.
2 Ibid.
3 Barrington Moore, Jr., *Social Origins of Dictatorship and Democracy: Lord and Peasant in the Making of the Modern World*, London: Allen Lane, 1967, p. 196.
4 *Argus* (Cape Town), 18 July 1991.
5 *Cape Times* (Cape Town), 8 August 1991.
6 *Financial Mail* (Johannesburg), 26 June 1992.
7 Adam Przeworski, *Democracy and the Market*, Cambridge: Cambridge University Press, 1991, p. 36.
8 Alexander Hamilton, James Madison and John Jay, *The Federalist, or the New Constitution*, London: J.M. Dent, 1911, p. 252. (The quotation is from the 48th Paper, attributed to Madison.)
9 ANC National Conference, July 1991, Report, p. 39.
10 Ibid., p. 34.
11 Marina Ottaway, 'Liberation movements and transition to democracy: the case of the ANC', *Journal of Modern African Studies*, vol. 29, no. 1 (1991), pp. 66–7; cf. Yunus Carrim, 'The ANC as a mass political organisation', in Alexander Johnstone, Sipho Shezi and Gavin Bradshaw (eds), *Constitution-making in the New South Africa*, London: Leicester University Press, 1993, pp. 108–9.
12 *Argus* (Cape Town), 26 November 1993.
13 Quoted in Hugh Murray, 'The long journey of Thabo Mbeki', *Leadership*, vol. 12, no. 4 (1993), p. 36.
14 *Argus* (Cape Town), 26 November 1993.

15 Quoted in *Rapport* (Johannesburg), 24 October 1993.

16 Quoted by an opposition spokesman (and not denied) in Debates of Parliament, 17 September 1993, col. 13084 (translation).

17 Jan Mellet, 'Die FW-Raaisel', *Insig* (Johannesburg), March 1993, pp. 20–21.

18 *Rapport* (Johannesburg), 12 September 1993.

19 *Die Burger* (Cape Town), 15 October 1993.

20 *Rapport* (Johannesburg), 31 October 1993.

21 Statement issued by Information Service of Bophuthatswana, 15 November 1993.

22 *Financial Mail* (Johannesburg), 3 December 1993.

23 *Argus* (Cape Town), 26 November 1993.

24 *Financial Mail*, (Johannesburg), 3 December 1993.

25 *Die Burger* (Cape Town), 4 December 1993.

26 Ibid., 18 November 1993.

27 Minister of Home Affairs, Debates of Parliament, 16 September 1993, col. 12928.

28 Chris de Kock, Cosmas Mareka, Nic Rhoodie and Charl Schutte, *The Prospects for a Free, Democratic Election*, Pretoria: Human Sciences Research Council. Data quoted as from pp. 18, 23, 25, 35 and 27.

3

SOUTH AFRICA'S DEFENCE AND SECURITY FORCES: THE NEXT DECADE

WILLIAM GUTTERIDGE

Introduction

The progressive adaptation of South Africa's defence and security forces to meet radically changed political conditions is essential if a relatively orderly transition to a new system of government is to be achieved. In the short term the success of the electoral process depends substantially on the conduct of these forces in the interim period and on the extent to which they are immediately able to contribute to the development of mutual trust between the various parties which will eventually form the new government. The same applies in the longer term to the finalization and full implementation of a definitive new constitution, a process which could last into the next century with a continuing struggle to achieve a balance of power by peaceful means.

The essential paradox is that while the government of South Africa has to be legitimized in the eyes of the majority of the population through the working of a democratic constitution, the defence, security and police forces have themselves to acquire or attract a kind of instant legitimacy in order to exercise the control which will make that possible.

In these circumstances it is not surprising that the debate on the military and security implications of political reform initially focused almost exclusively on the 'ad hoc' arrangements for the establishment under the auspices of the Transitional Executive Council of a method of joint or multi-party control. It is self-evident not only that these arrangements could anticipate or pre-empt the work of the constitution-makers but that they will be a key element in the confidence-building process.

For example, those involved in the sub-councils for defence or law and order have little alternative but to assume the continuation, at least for the time being, of the existing role of the South African Defence Force (SADF) in internal security in support of the civil power. That may, however, be seen to prejudice a radical long-term review of the means of managing riot and civil disorder and the possibility of, for instance, extending nationwide the existing Internal Stability Units (ISUs) into a paramilitary force or forces, which would perhaps be directly account-able, along with the police, to regional administrations. This was, inci-dentally, a good practical argument for an early decision about the fields of responsibility of regional governments. There are, however, other reasons than immediate political expediency or convenience for consid-ering the long-term restructuring of South Africa's armed forces now. 'Ad hoc' adjustments and arrangements which have been made are essential for a real sharing of responsibility for security between National Party, ANC, Homeland (TVBC) and other leaderships, and for coopera-tion to combat violence at local levels. The continuing efficiency of such measures will, however, be enhanced if at an early stage (preferably before the election) there can be a decision in something more than principle about the ultimate defence requirements of the 'new South Africa' and the shape and character of the armed forces to match.

Defence requirements by the turn of the century

An initial review of defence needs initiated soon after President de Klerk came to office quickly resulted in a reduction of defence expenditure from 4.2 per cent to 2.6 per cent of GDP.[1] Early steps included the reduction of initial military service from two years to one and the closing of certain bases: by the fourth quarter of 1993 the total number of military aircraft in service was cut from 800 to 450. These reductions were essentially a 'peace dividend' resulting from the end of the Angolan war, the independence of Namibia and improved relations with other neighbouring states following the virtual withdrawal of the Soviet Union from the region.

The dramatic change in the geopolitical circumstances in itself de-manded a far-reaching reassessment of South Africa's defence needs. It is not just that the conventional threat in Southern Africa has virtually vanished. At the same time the precision and destructive power of weapons based on the latest technology have reduced the quantity required and correspondingly the number of military personnel to man them. In other words, the new South Africa requires a much smaller but technically more sophisticated defence force for deterrent purposes.

Consequently, although for the time being the size and composition of South Africa's armed forces will inevitably be determined by political factors, not least the need to keep existing personnel occupied and relatively content, objective analysis of more strictly military considerations has to take place quickly: indeed is already taking place. During 1993, in fact, the SADF established the basis of a formal strategic management process. Professionally the most sensitive area is the balance between ground, air and maritime forces within the SADF itself. A minimum deterrent force to defend the territorial integrity of the state against the emergence of a notional aggressor might consist of a reduced air force comprising perhaps three squadrons of fighter bombers, plus helicopters and a few transport aircraft in support of a ground force of two or three brigades with armoured personnel carriers and mobile heavy artillery but not tanks. Senior air force staff have reluctantly come to the conclusion that a single squadron of supersonic fighters might provide an adequate nucleus for expansion if the situation deteriorated and that South Africa might not be able to afford anything more. Sceptics including the ANC(MK) have, perhaps understandably, some reservations about such a minimalist approach by professionals. However, the debate on this issue has so far been reassuringly rational and objective. In any case, a replacement programme for outdated major equipment is now urgent and, given the constraints of a reduced defence budget, is a priority for long-term planning: this applies most pressingly to the Impala aircraft. Regional and other possible strategic requirements could dictate a revived and enlarged navy and prompt a general redesign of the SADF.

The prospect of developing a cooperative Southern African regional system of security based on non-military networks such as power supply, transport and water is regarded in some quarters as attractive, but there is a strong resistance by neighbouring states to becoming more economically dependent on South Africa than they already are. However, initiatives to develop regional peacekeeping and disaster forces may help attract outside interest and assistance which could redound to South Africa's advantage. The development of internal community service battalions is in any case a likely way of dispersing surplus military manpower.

Growing consensus

Since February 1992, when the question of private armies was first raised in CODESA, a remarkable degree of consensus appears to have developed between the South African government and the ANC on defence matters. This has inevitably been punctuated by aggressive public rhetoric, for instance disparaging remarks about the size and quality of Umkhonto we Sizwe (MK) on the one side and about alleged undercover activities by existing SADF personnel on the other, but overall there has been a recognition of extensive common ground.

Papers and speeches emanating from the Ministry of Defence and the SADF on the one hand and from the ANC(MK) and the Military Research Group on the other display an encouraging convergence of thinking on general principles. While there are indications of some divisions within ANC circles about restricting the size and even determining the orientation of armed forces on idealistic rather than ideological grounds, it is likely that the pragmatists who are primarily interested in the power and authority of the new state will prevail. There is a realistic complementary appreciation on both sides of the risks of encouraging readily politicized armed forces.

Contrary to expectations, especially after the impasse in CODESA in mid-1992, the military question proved during 1993 surprisingly amenable to negotiation. That this was so manifestly depended on the leading personalities in both the SADF and MK.

Joe Modise, long-standing Commander of Umkhonto we Sizwe, ultimately emerged as a pragmatist with a keen understanding of military issues. This was recognized by his opposite numbers in the SADF, who in their turn progressively attracted his respect as blunt professionals. First, Lt.-Gen. 'Kat' Liebenberg, at one time Commander of the Special Forces, and then, following an appointment which surprised many because of his harsh public criticism of the ANC, Lt.-Gen. George Meiring quickly adapted to the shifting demands of the political situation. The latter's assumption of the command of the SADF in November 1993, on the retirement of his predecessor, was evidently a recognition of the fact that problems of integration were likely to prove marginal in parts of the Defence Force other than the army.

The percolation of the increasing consensus down to the middle ranks of the army in particular was assisted by the realization that the scale of the short-term problem with regard to MK was small and that its leaders at least understood the implications of their demand for 'affirmative action'.

Common ground

The fundamentals of a national defence policy, according to the assertion by the Minister of Defence in parliament on 1 June 1993, are unlikely to be changed under a Government of National Unity, or any successor. In the terms stated, and in the light of the ANC's known views, this seems a reasonable claim. South Africa has no territorial ambitions or aggressive intentions and favours conflict resolution rather than confrontation and will take military action only in the face of direct threat to its interests when other measures have failed. The SADF will, it seems to be agreed, project a credible conventional deterrent ability as an African regional force, if necessary using mobile forces in a tactically offensive mode. It is accepted that expenditure on defence will be affected by social priorities: SADF medical services will be available to the police and prison services and to assist community development.

There is also a clear consensus amongst those directly concerned about the principles governing any assimilation, incorporation, merger or accommodation of the various existing military and paramilitary forces in the defence forces. It seems to be accepted that the Defence Force and its personnel are to be non-partisan, apolitical, loyal to the constitution and responsible to the government of the day. Discrimination on the basis of race, colour, gender or religion will be prohibited, and appointment and promotion will be based on professional military criteria, maintaining standards of proficiency. The rights of serving individuals will be subject to the Military Discipline Code and they will have to respect the agreed Code of Conduct, which has been on the table for some time.

These principles were largely embodied in the TEC legislation enacted during the September 1993 session of parliament. During the debate on 14 September the Minister of Defence, Kobie Coetzee, announced that when the current year's white national servicemen had completed their one-year initial call-up, a non-racial essentially volunteer system would be introduced. If there were insufficient volunteers, the requirement would be met by a ballot system drawing on the relevant age group. All males reaching Standard 10 educationally (the final year of compulsory schooling) will have to register up to the age of 26. Already the introduction of two-year voluntary service for the permanent force was bridging the gap, and other volunteers were starting basic training which will maintain the continuity of the part-time citizen force component.

While it can probably be safely assumed that agreement on such matters as eventual force levels, equipment and related operational matters connected with external defence will be relatively easily achieved, there is obviously much scope for essentially political controversy about the practical arrangements reflecting these unexceptionable general principles. Non-discrimination is easy to assert but difficult to exercise and even more difficult to prove to those who believe themselves victimized or discriminated against. Such key elements as the domestic role, function and ethos or orientation will be finally resolved only when a new government is in place. It is not clear whether there is agreement on what many senior SADF officers seem to regard as desirable – namely the progressive withdrawal of the military from its recently intensified role in support of the police.

There are a number of issues which will have to be resolved over time but obviously cannot be ignored even before the election. Will there be affirmative action to redress the imbalances of personnel from different population groups: if so, what will be its character? Is it generally accepted (as has been affirmed in current government circles) that only part of the defence force will continue to be full-time, with an adequate reserve? Will the existing regimental and unit structure of the citizen force be retained? What checks and balances, if any, will be instituted to discourage any tendency to intervention in politics; and if a regimental system is retained, will it be on a strictly geographical or other basis? The institutions and processes, such as selection and training, necessary to create national armed forces for the new South Africa have either to be created from scratch within months, or evolved from what is already in place and then authenticated or legitimized in the eyes of potential users.

Defence forces in the transitional phase

In the meantime, the relative effectiveness of transitional arrangements for joint command and control in managing violence will be important in determining the ultimate status of the armed forces within the new constitution. Any consequent success in assimilating the disparate military elements into a single, full representative national army, could be a significant contribution towards nation-building and resultant stability.

Joint control

Effective exercise of joint control over the defence and security forces during the transitional phase is essential not only for operational reasons but as a confidence-building measure. The perception that the process is working is more important than adherence to strict bureaucratic procedures. It was never going to be easy for the ANC to accept responsibility and therefore blame for internal security operations, and always likely that the SADF would be inclined to blame errors and failures on the dilution of their professional standards from outside.

However, once the concept of joint control had been accepted at the political level, with the creation of sub-councils for defence, policing and separately for intelligence and the entrenchment of a form of civilian control through a defence secretariat, then the key to success lay in a military high command, with a Joint Coordinating Committee, and in the interaction of the personalities of the Chairman of the Sub-council and the Commander of the SADF.

The first essential step was for all existing military or paramilitary forces to be under one command and political control. The initial criterion for this is important, namely the willingness on the part of such forces to subordinate themselves to a central authority. In principle at least this could extend beyond the SADF, MK and the TVBC forces to the Azanian People's Liberation Army (APLA) or even to the Afrikaner Resistance Movement (AWB). The numerous MK cadres still outside the country may continue to present a problem in this respect, especially in view of the cost of repatriating them. Public debate about a merger with the SADF has in the event proved premature and to some extent an obstacle to early agreement on joint control – an example of the way in which oversimplification and dramatization of the various issues has complicated what are inevitably difficult negotiations.

Merger or assimilation: options for change
Once the various military forces are effectively under joint command, rationalization and a degree of integration will have to take place. This will involve assessment and selection and in a general sense discrimination in order to achieve as rapidly as possible greater representation for black people, particularly at the different levels of the military hierarchy.

In terms of numbers in relation to the existing establishment of the SADF (see box) the problem does not appear overwhelming. The TVBC defence forces (each with a miniature air wing) are apparently small:[2]

Transkei	2,000 +	Bophuthatswana	3,000 +
Venda	1,000 +	Ciskei	1,000 +

Total ANC cadres are estimated at a maximum of about 10,000, with possibly as few as 4,500 within the boundaries of South Africa. An upper

---

South Africa's total armed forces, 1993

ACTIVE: 67,500; *of which* 6,000 Medical Services; 35,400 white conscripts; 4,200 women.

RESERVES: 360,000 Citizen Force; 135,000 Active Citizen Force Reserve; ~140,000 Commandos.

ARMY: ~47,000. Full Time Force: 18,000; *of which* 12,000 white; 4,000 black and Coloured; 2,000 women.

NAVY: ~4,500; *of which* ~900 conscripts; ~300 women.

AIR FORCE: 10,000; *of which* 3,000 conscripts; ~400 women

PARAMILITARY: 110,000 South African Police; 37,000 Police Reserves

---

~ estimated.

Source: *The Military Balance 1993–1994*, London: Brassey's for the International Institute for Strategic Studies, 1993, pp. 217–18.

Note: Recent changes in South African policy, including the reduction in military service and the suspension of white conscription, mean these figures are now only an approximation of the current position.

limit of 20,000 in all for these forces does not on the face of it present an overwhelming problem, given an SADF with its permanent cadre recently reduced to between 50,000 and 60,000, and with a total for the reserve and commando units of around 400,000 – mainly white of all ages.

Apart from the placing of senior officers at appropriate positions in the military hierarchy and the swift training and absorption of suitably educated officers in the middle ranks of the national defence force, it may be wise, at least as a temporary measure, to regard the TVBC's independent homeland forces as embryonic contingents within an internal security role. This appears to be the accepted policy, though even Venda's force of 1,000 to 1,500 men might prove too large for this purpose. It may be appropriate to transfer a few key senior officers directly into the national command structure in order to assert the intention of achieving national unity. New roles for them could be identified initially on a temporary basis.

Whether assimilation takes place on an individual or occasionally on a sub-unit basis, the primary objective is to avoid disaffection on all sides, while creating conditions conducive to cooperation in maintaining order. Redundant white colonels and majors, whose careers and pension rights have been blighted, and unemployed or otherwise unoccupied former 'freedom fighters' both have a potential to subvert or disrupt the process of change.

There is a strong case for attempting to find alternative civil employment for 'military' cadres which are not otherwise required. The possibility of forming units for community service has already been mentioned. Taking a longer-term view, SADF and ANC(MK) commanders are already contemplating a type of non-military national service in the form of a Peace Corps in an effort to retrieve what is rather patronizingly termed 'the lost generation'. Means of subsidizing or encouraging commercial and industrial companies to find employment for individuals near to their home ground is one method which has been tried with some success in northern Mozambique. Integration into commando units in some politically suitable areas could also be considered. Though a relatively small dissident radical element is likely to remain unassimilable, the commonplace human desire for the majority to identify and belong will probably prevail. This is where, particularly as the defence force is refined in size and organization over the next few years and individuals are discharged or pensioned off, traditional regimental welfare organizations could play a useful reassuring role by involving families and dependents.

In this interim stage, particularly over the next year, sensitive improvisation of procedures and organizations will predominate. At the same time decisions about the longer-term shape of the armed forces, the intelligence services and the police will be taken and implemented.

Some active coordination will be necessary to ensure that progressive reconciliation of short-term development needs and long-term reorganization is achieved. This could be the responsibility of, for example, a Council for Defence with a broadly based membership and perhaps the participation of neutral observers. In any case, some means of exercising an overview at a high level is essential in order first to establish the rationale and ethos of the reconstructed forces and security services and then to implement and put into practice revised and expanded organizations with appropriate education and training programmes.

The institution of a National Peacekeeping Force (NPKF) to maintain law and order during the transitional phase could, apart from its immediate utility, pave the way for a permanent paramilitary force for internal security. Whether or not in practice it actually takes the place of the units of the SADF normally on standby to cope with civil disturbance, the aim is for it to be roughly equivalent in terms of numbers; but it seems likely to be much smaller than the 10,000 soldiers who until recently have been

habitually on standby. Comprising elements drawn from
brought under joint control, possibly including the KwaZulu ᵽ
subject to assessment and retraining on an individual basis. G
the participation of Internal Stability Units from the South
Police, the foundations of a paramilitary force are then establi. .ᴧu at
least for an experimental period and short- or longer-term needs are on
the way to reconciliation. The brevity of the transitional period means the
NPKF's value is likely to be symbolic rather than operational, but even
so it will be an important confidence-building measure.

Doctrines and practice for the next decade

As already suggested, South Africa's need for a defence force into the
twenty-first century is related to three roles:

(1) Deterrence of any possible external threat to the state's territorial
integrity.
(2) Frontier control and border protection including the potential
control of refugee flows and migration into South Africa arising
from instability in neighbouring countries, and related threats such
as drug trafficking and the spread of AIDS.
(3) Internal security operations in support of the police, in aid of the
civil power.

Either or both of the second and third functions could be transferred
exclusively to a paramilitary force or gendarmerie, but it can be assumed
that the military will continue for the time being to be involved in both
these functions, at least as a last resort.

The phasing out of white conscription and the need to shift the balance
of the racial and ethnic composition of the defence force towards the
black population raise the broad question of manpower procurement as
well as the potential issue of ethos and orientation.

Military ethos: a coup-proof army?

None of the various parties involved in the negotiations intended to lead
to the creation of a democratic South Africa has a proven recipe for an
apolitical defence force able and willing to respect and defend the
constitution of a democratic state.

While the professional culture of the existing SADF is manifestly
derived from the British tradition, it has in practice given more or less

unquestioning allegiance to one political party for over forty years. The TVBC forces, though starting in the same tradition, have followed the example of the armies of many of the former colonial states in sub-Saharan Africa and intervened in politics. The ANC's MK in its turn has been trained mainly in a mixture of Marxist-Leninist, Maoist and other military doctrines and techniques.

The possibility of a military coup in South Africa has been touted for a decade on the assumption that there would come a time when right-wing elements within and outside the SADF would combine to thwart a National Party committed to radical reform and an eventual transfer of power. Most expert observers agree that a coup in the classic sense of a seizure of power nationwide is unlikely to be feasible in a country the size of South Africa, with centres of power of one kind or another in three or four major cities a long way apart. It would, for instance, be difficult to mobilize, concentrate and arm reservists in adequate numbers. On the other hand, after what could well be classified as a potential armed insurrection by the Afrikaner Volksfront movement at the World Trade Centre in Johannesburg on 25 June 1993, it would be unwise not to take into account the possibility of an army or police mutiny – an action such as the Curragh mutiny in 1914 which thwarted Britain's Irish policy.

Now, however, there is much more concern on the part even of those who dismiss the idea of a white right-wing coup that the restructuring of the composition of South Africa's defence forces under a government of national unity could lead to the assimilation of large contingents of black soldiers, with political or tribal allegiances, who would pose a corresponding threat especially to the democratic process and a coalition government. The Angolan experience has not done much to alleviate these fears, though the success in creating new Namibian defence forces could have done so.

This convergence of fears has created a somewhat naive obsession with the idea of a 'coup-proof' as opposed to a coup-prone army. Historically this has proved to be an illusion. In Ethiopia, for example, the former Emperor Haile Selassie deliberately attempted to select and train an officer corps to ensure continuity. In the event he was deposed by Marxist revolutionaries from its ranks. On the other hand, Indira Gandhi was on record as suggesting that the army had remained neutral and not intervened in India largely because of the size of the subcontinent, the army's ethnic regimental diversity and balance, and especially India's hundred-year-old democratic political culture.

The African experience as a whole is discouraging but consistent. The key countries of former British and French Africa which inherited small colonial armies of proven quality intervened in most cases not at all because of any inherent tendency but because of the failure of political leaders to produce results, an excessive centralization of power and the lack of well-rooted political culture. It is relevant to the South African debate about military allegiance, political control and accountability that the Ghanaian Colonel A.A. Afrifa, one of the coup leaders who later became head of state,[3] claimed in his book *The Ghana Coup 24th February 1966* that at the time he and his colleagues were acting to defend the country's constitution. The intention was to stop the misuse and abuse of power by President Kwame Nkrumah and to restore freedom and civil rights to the population. The book has even been described as 'a challenging defence of democracy',[4] but the action of Afrifa and his colleagues could also be defined as an attempt at preserving the constitution by the ultimately unconstitutional instrument – a military coup.

These references are made not, of course, to suggest a model but to avoid a futile search for a simplistic solution to a complex and subtle problem. Apart from a continuing and deliberate effort to support the development of the political conventions necessary for sustenance of a democratic system and thus provide a civilized framework within which the military can operate, the most obvious structural step is to work quickly towards an ethnic, racial and tribal balance within the defence force and even within its units and formations. In this respect the model of the former British Indian Army has stood the test of time, including a prolonged state of emergency. It is significant that the origins of its success undoubtedly lay in impartial external assistance, with initial officer education and training, advanced technical training and programmes for command and staff advancement which from the first integrated all three of the armed services into the international professional military tradition of democratic societies.

Implementing conversion and change

The realization of the twin objectives of a secure defence for South Africa and security forces compatible with a democracy and a government of national unity depends initially on *a series of decisions in principle* concerning:

(1) The overall role and functions of the military, including interservice relations.

(2) Internal security responsibilities and mechanisms for initiating action in the aid of the civil power, the limits to such action and the line of accountability.

(3) The composition of the army, achievement of an ethnic and racial balance with or without a fixed quota system, and raised either by selective conscription with a small professional cadre or on an all-volunteer basis.

(4) The relationship between defence arrangements and the structure of government, and the extent of decentralization to regions.

(5) The deliberate determination of an ethos or philosophy for the defence force aimed at rendering it apolitical and democratically accountable.

All these are questions for which the participation of a variety of international experts may be desirable not only in the interests of balance and impartiality, but in the search for the best solution. Sanctions, boycotts and the arms embargo have inevitably tended to isolate the South African military from recent developments in doctrine and training. The involvement of external advisers or observers within what must be an essentially South African process will speed up the country's reintegration into the international community and even provide a basis for formal regional cooperation in a security system.

Training and selection practicalities
New and expanded training programmes are now immediately required, including:

(1) Conversion courses to train newly assimilated personnel from MK and other military elements for service in a national defence force.

(2) Retraining and reorientation courses for existing SADF personnel to enable them to adjust to the new circumstances.

(3) Joint programmes of training to develop cooperation and understanding between the different elements and cadres.

(4) The establishment of training facilities to cope with the new 'volunteer' force.

(5) The expansion of the existing military academy to accommodate longer courses and accelerate 'Africanization'.

It is at these points that there is the most obvious role for international supervision and monitoring through direct participation in training, beginning with the planning of programmes and syllabuses. Without this, acceptable change in ethos and orientation is unlikely to be achieved.

Avoiding even the appearance of discrimination without a referee, judge, umpire, arbitrator, facilitator or honest broker is always likely to be very difficult. This applies especially to the determination of educational and other qualifications, to processes of selection and promotion, and to all kinds of command and staff training. The necessary expansion of the relevant academies, colleges and training schools is likely to prove almost impossible without discreet external assistance, at least for validating purposes. Validation in order to demonstrate good faith in South African circumstances seems more appropriate than an introduction of foreign training teams as such.

Advanced flying training and other activities involving obviously high levels of technical skill are *ipso facto* less susceptible to charges of discrimination and partiality. Military and civil requirements for pilots and technicians could be met at one and the same time. This is an area in which overseas training might even predominate, but ideally there might be a facility to serve the whole of Southern Africa. However, at different levels in other fields international assistance can play a key, even vital, role. Certainly a network of exchanges and placements for staff and com-mand training at military academies and staff colleges overseas should be quickly established. There has been little resistance to the restoration of this convention. At initial officer training level, such as that provided by Britain at the Royal Military Academy, Sandhurst, the overseas experience of a small number of young officers from a wide range of African and Asian countries has over a long period provided a useful benchmark and means of assay for internal training. It is certainly the case that there is virtue in having some variety of source for these kinds of assistance. The essential conditions, however, are that the sources should be homogeneous in terms of language and professional ethos and that they should not recently have been affected in any way by social, ethnic or particularly political tensions of any kind. By no means all the leading democracies are relatively immune from such issues. For South Africa an increasingly important consideration is likely to be the development of regional cooperation and the rehabilitation of armed forces in neighbouring states. The stability and attractiveness to investors of the whole Southern African region are likely to depend substantially on the decisions South Africa is now taking about its defence and security forces. There is thus mutual advantage in inviting assistance particularly from European countries with existing economic and strategic interests in South Africa and its neighbours.

The time factor, however, remains critical if South Africa is simultaneously to put in place the means of national peacekeeping for the next two or three years, while the new constitution is implemented, and to begin to accept the responsibilities of being a major regional power.

Notes

This paper is a product of the continuing project of the Research Institute for the Study of Conflict and Terrorism on the future of South Africa's defence and security forces. RISCT gratefully acknowledges all the support it has received, especially two grants from the Dulverton Trust.

1 Conference paper by Lt.-Gen. P.D. Steyn, Chief of Defence Force Staff, SADF, Pretoria, 22 April 1993.
2 These figures are based on *The Military Balance 1993–1994*, London: Brassey's for the International Institute for Strategic Studies, 1993, p. 219, and on other, confidential sources.
3 The author of this chapter, incidentally, taught Afrifa throughout his time at the Royal Military Academy at Sandhurst.
4 Dr K.A. Busia, concluding the Preface of Afrifa's book, Frank Cass: London, 1966, p. 10.

4

THE SOUTH AFRICAN ECONOMY: PROBLEMS AND PROSPECTS

CHARLES SIMKINS

Introduction

The South African economy is currently emerging from its worst recession since the 1930s. From October 1989 to December 1992, real GDP growth was negative during every quarter except the third quarter of 1991. Against a backdrop of population growth still in excess of 2 per cent per annum, this has meant a sharp decline in the average living standard.

The reasons for this very poor performance can be grouped into three categories:

(1) *conjunctural factors*, including the effects of difficult international economic conditions and extensive drought at home;
(2) *structural factors* of long standing, many of which account for the poor performance of the South African economy since the mid-1970s, and which have been exacerbated by a low gold price and poor commodity prices in recent years;
(3) *political factors*, whose effects can be traced through the imposition of trade and financial sanctions during the 1980s and the consequent sapping of private-sector confidence.

There are signs that the situation is starting to improve. Real GDP increased in the first half of 1993, owing largely to improved agricultural conditions. Both the South African Reserve Bank's coincident economic indicator and the South African Chamber of Business's business confidence index[1] suggest that the economy had bottomed out by mid-1993. Third-quarter estimates for 1993 (GDP growth in excess of 8 per cent in annualized terms) indicated that the improvement was spreading to

65

sectors other than agriculture and accelerating more rapidly than expected earlier in the year.[2]

Changes in the economic landscape

Savings and investment

Gross domestic fixed investment as a proportion of GDP dropped to the lowest level ever recorded (since 1946) and stood at 16 per cent in the third quarter of 1992.[3] It continued to decline in the first half of 1993, though the rate of decrease then slowed. This compares with an average ratio of 23.5 per cent in the 1980s. The drop is ominous, especially in the context of rising capital intensity in the economy over the past twenty years. Many believe that net fixed investment is now close to zero; the estimates of depreciation of the capital stock in the national accounts indicate such a conclusion. The causes seem clear enough: low levels of domestic and international demand, low levels of capacity utilization, political uncertainty and application of domestic savings to the repayment of foreign debt.

There has also been a drop in savings, which fell from 23.5 per cent of GDP in the third quarter of 1989 to 16.5 per cent in 1992.[4] An important component in this development was the behaviour of general government, which has been a net dissaver since 1984. By the second quarter of 1993, the rate had risen to 17.5 per cent, as the combined result of a rise in the net saving of the private sector and a decline in the net dissaving of general government.

In the late 1980s, an excess of savings over investment made it possible to repay foreign debt, but the capacity to do so was eroded in the early 1990s and a further agreement with foreign creditors has recently been concluded.

The South African economy can be characterized as one which needs to shift resources from consumption to investment, in both the private and the public sectors. The required shift is substantial. Through endorsement of the government's Normative Economic Model, the Minister of Finance has proposed investment targets of an additional 3 per cent of GNP in the public sector and a further 5 per cent of GNP in the private sector.[5] Even if the target growth rate of 3.6 per cent per annum associated with these proposals is met, the shift from consumption to investment would mean austerity for the rest of the decade.

Cutting across the proposals of the Normative Economic Model (whose central concerns are an increase in exports and investment) are emerging proposals to finance a *reconstruction programme*, the core elements of which are housing, improvement of urban infrastructure, land reform, rural development and education. The private sector (through the Platform for Investment studies[6]), the Development Bank of Southern Africa and the ANC's Macroeconomic Research Group have all been working on this issue and reports will be released which will affect the debate in the run-up to the April 1994 elections. It is already clear that there is a wide range of opinions on priorities, sequencing and the way in which the economy will react to new policies.

Monetary and fiscal policy
The South African Reserve Bank sets guidelines for the broadly defined money supply aggregate M3. The lower limit guideline was set at 7 per cent and the upper limit at 10 per cent at the beginning of 1992 and reset at 6 per cent and 9 per cent respectively at the beginning of 1993. M3 remained within the guidelines during 1992, but fell well below them by actually contracting slightly in the first half of 1993. During this period, the private sector shifted from longer-term to shorter-term deposits with banks, thereby increasing its liquidity.

The stated objective of *monetary policy* is to protect the internal and external value of the rand. Up to mid-1992, little effect could be detected in respect of the Consumer Price Index (CPI), though by then the Producer Price Index (PPI) had started to fall. From late 1992, however, the inflation rate fell from 15 per cent (the average level for the entire period since the mid-1970s) to below 10 per cent by mid-1993. The most recently reported annual rate of increase in the PPI is 5.5 per cent.[7] A number of observers are projecting a further fall in the CPI – to around 7 per cent – by mid-1994. These changes have taken place despite an increase in the rate of Value Added Tax from 10 per cent to 14 per cent at the beginning of April 1993, which caused only a minor and temporary upward 'blip' in the CPI.

Greater pressure can be detected in the field of *fiscal policy*. The government's estimated deficit for 1992/93 at the time of the introduction of the annual budget in March was 4.1 per cent of GDP. A year later, the revised estimate for that year had risen to 8.6 per cent. The 1993/94 budget planned a deficit of 6.8 per cent, or just over R25 billion,* to be financed mainly from the sale of domestic stock. Most commentators

*About £4.54 billion, given a conversion rate of approximately 5.5 rand to the pound sterling.

regard the budget as mildly stimulatory; the limitation of the deficit to 6.8 per cent is intended to create scope for a gradually more relaxed monetary policy approach. High public-sector borrowing requirements have not put noticeable upward pressure on interest rates, which have been declining in nominal terms since late 1992. This reflects low private-sector demand for investment finance. Economic recovery will change the parameters; it is important that private investment should not be crowded out by government dissaving.

Apart from the increase in VAT, the main tax innovation was a decrease of the company tax rate from 48 per cent to 40 per cent, along with the introduction of a tax of 15 per cent on all income from companies that is distributed in dividends. This measure was designed to stimulate self-financing of new investment by companies.

Taxation will be a major political issue for some years to come. One debate is the relative contributions of direct and indirect tax to total tax revenue. This fell from 45.7 per cent in 1988/89 to 39.9 per cent in 1992/93. The trend was reversed in the 1993/94 budget, in terms of which the ratio should rise to 43.3 per cent. The government would like to see the ratio rise further, but it is running into resistance, chiefly from the trade unions. The increase in VAT had to be accompanied by continued zero-rating of basic foods, although the International Monetary Fund (IMF) correctly argued that it would be better in principle not to zero-rate, but for the government to apply funds directly to the alleviation of poverty. An increase in the fuel levy in October 1993 also provoked resistance and was partially reversed.

A second debate is over whether there should be a special reconstruction levy (as compensation for unjust enrichment of part of the population resulting from conquest, segregation and apartheid, and to finance a reconstruction programme) and, if so, what form it should take. Some have suggested a wealth tax. At present, there are two main taxes on wealth – property rates, which accrue to municipalities, and estate duties. Both these taxes are likely to rise. Property rates will be under pressure as racially segregated municipalities are united. Estate duty is low, with a million-rand exemption and a flat rate of 15 per cent. It could easily be increased. Other forms of wealth tax would be more difficult to introduce. They would require a lot more information to be collected by the Department of Inland Revenue and they could have substantial effects on asset portfolios, *inter alia* triggering off a further round of capital flight.

Institutional aspects of fiscal policy also need to be considered. Attempts are being made to gain greater control over state expenditure. One important trend in recent years has been poor control of increasing deficits in the second and third tiers of black government. There is hardly a black local authority in the country whose revenue is sufficient to meet its recurrent costs, let alone service its debt. And both the self-governing territories and the TBVC 'states' have run up substantial debts with little prospect of repayment. Recently, the central government was obliged to intervene directly to contain spiralling salary expenditure in Lebowa. A complicated effort to retrieve the situation is under way, involving the Department of Foreign Affairs and the Development Bank of Southern Africa. But the situation is not likely to be fully under control for some time. There have also been frequent reports of maladmini-stration and corruption within central government, increasing fruitless expenditure.

Balance of payments
The balance of trade usually improves during a recession; this improve-ment eventually creates room for higher levels of domestic expendi-ture. However, the surplus on the current account of the balance of payments (seasonally adjusted and annualized) deteriorated from R11.9 billion in the fourth quarter of 1991 to R0.7 billion in the first quarter of 1993. During 1992, the effects of severe drought curtailed agricultural exports and necessitated a sharp increase in agricultural imports. Also, the gold price was not particularly favourable for much of the year. The current account balance strengthened markedly in the second quarter of 1993, largely as a result of a sharp rise in the value of merchandise exports and a moderate rise in the value of gold exports.

The net outflow of capital started to increase in the second quarter of 1992 and reached R3.7 billion in the first quarter of 1993. This can partly be attributed to political factors (stalled negotiations and then the Hani assassination). The Reserve Bank also reported a considerable switching from foreign to domestic trade financing in the third quarter of 1992, ascribing this to the relatively favourable costs of domestic credit. Short-term capital movements accounted for most of these developments. In the second quarter of 1993, the net outflow of capital declined; along with the surplus on the current balance, this strengthened the net gold and other foreign reserves by R1.2 billion. However, figures from the Reserve Bank's December 1993 *Quarterly Bulletin* show that net capital outflow peaked at an unexpected R5.3 billion in the third quarter. The real exchange rate, having fluctuated within a narrow range in 1991 and 1992, depreciated by 4.9 per cent in the first half of 1993. In October

1993, it was possible for the authorities to arrest and slightly reverse the nominal depreciation of the rand against sterling and the dollar.

The foreign reserves position remains weak. A decline of R2.3 billion in 1992 was followed by a further decrease of R2.0 billion in the first half of 1993. The government target of three months' import cover is far from being met at present, and observers, especially press and business economists, have commented that foreign reserves have never been so low at the start of an economic upswing. Some hope can be pinned on improvements in the capital account, especially if confidence is not undermined prior to the elections. The capital account will be helped, both directly and indirectly, by the successful negotiation of a US$850 million loan from the IMF at the end of 1993. Recovery in the international economy may also assist export growth. But it appears that the balance of payments will continue to hinder economic recovery.

Drops in domestic inflation and in European interest rates have permitted drops in South African short-term and capital market rates. The bank rate was cut from 15 per cent to 14 per cent in November 1992; and further cuts of 1 per cent each were made in February and October 1993. A further drop is, however, unlikely before the elections.

Employment
Under the circumstances outlined above, the employment picture looks grim. Total employment in the non-agricultural sectors of the economy declined in ten of the fifteen quarters up to the fourth quarter of 1992. The overall rate of decline in non-agricultural employment was close to 3 per cent in 1992. Over the past few years, government employment has risen fairly steadily. From an index of 100 in 1985, it rose to 105 at the beginning of 1988 and stood at 107 at the end of 1992.[8] By contrast, private formal sector employment (excluding agriculture and domestic service) has been hard hit; from an index of 100 in 1985, it rose to 103 at the end of 1989, but had declined to 95 by the end of 1992. Despite these developments, the rate of increase in the average monthly remuneration per worker in the non-agricultural sectors of the economy declined only modestly, from 18 per cent in 1989 to 15.2 per cent in 1992. Real wages per worker have actually risen in recent years; the real increase in 1992 was 2.6 per cent. Labour productivity has also risen, principally as a result of retrenchments, but at a lower rate, pushing up unit labour costs.

It is impossible to discuss employment in *agriculture* with much certainty, because information in this area (itself of uncertain quality) is published several years in arrears. However, agricultural workers must have been hard hit by the 1991/92 drought, with the considerable army of casual workers taking the brunt of the effect on employment. Full-time agricultural workers probably suffered a real drop in wages. Self-employed farmers in the homelands would also have been affected by the drought, but in itself this would have had a small effect on household incomes. A number of surveys during the past decade have shown that most households in the homelands derive only a small part (usually less than a quarter) of their income from agriculture. The balance is made up of state transfers (particularly pensions – the real value of black pensions has risen in recent years, as a result of the elimination of the racial gap) and remittances from members of households working in urban areas.

Much interest has been shown in the *informal sector* in recent years. The pro-entrepreneurial, deregulatory emphases in the international economic debate of the 1980s have been taken up by both the private and the public sector in South Africa. Cities have removed restrictions on street trading and informal markets, and these activities have blossomed. Commuter transport between business districts and black residential areas has been revolutionized, with heavily subsidized large bus services being replaced in part by 'combi-taxis', which can carry twelve or fourteen passengers at a time, the routes varying according to their requirements.

It is likely that the contribution of the informal sector to the economy has grown in recent years, partly because of deregulation and partly because of a shift in the distribution of income towards black people. (However, the possibility of a shift towards the informal sector among whites – little considered in South African analysis – must be borne in mind, as households struggle to cope with declining real incomes.) Measuring the extent of value added and employment generated in this sector is always difficult. Two surveys were run by Central Statistical Services (CSS) among Coloured, Asian and black households, in October 1990 and October 1991. These suggest that at the beginning of the 1990s the informal sector added about 8 per cent to conventionally measured GNP. Average incomes (though widely dispersed) are well below unskilled wages in the formal sector, so that labour absorption in the informal sector is considerable. However, many workers in the informal sector use it as a second source of income or as a fill-in while waiting to find formal sector work. Many more regard themselves as 'not economically active' on the whole and simply participate in the informal sector on a sporadic or part-time basis. Most people work for themselves, though one finds informal sector enterprises with a few employees; some of these have the potential to grow.

Unfortunately, CSS surveys of the informal sector have not been integrated with earlier surveys measuring unemployment, so a full and coherent description of conditions in the labour market is not possible. It appears that the informal sector helps as far as labour absorption is concerned (as it has done for decades), but that it coexists with a high level of open unemployment. Moreover, informal sector activity closely depends on income generated in the formal sector and so is pro-cyclical in nature.

High levels of unemployment have prompted a discussion of a *public works programme* (PWP) among the short-term working group of the National Economic Forum. Much of the debate has been about the possibility of more labour-intensive techniques of infrastructural and housing construction, mainly in the urban areas, although should there be a relatively strong economic upswing some of this pressure may abate. There are difficulties with PWPs: in the first place, the state is in a poor position to finance them, though loans from individual countries or the World Bank might become available for the purpose. Secondly, it is clear that if a PWP is to have a substantial employment impact, the wages must be low – perhaps of the order of R200 per month. Such wages are much more likely to attract people in the rural areas than in the urban areas. Until recently, there has been no coherent rural development policy into which rural public works can fit. A World Bank report on land reform published in September 1993 suggests, however, that there is considerable scope for a grant-aided process of land acquisition by small farmers. Implicit in this would be a demand for rural infrastructural development. World Bank analysis of urban areas also stresses the importance of infrastructural development. But an urban PWP will face a more difficult labour supply position, not only because relatively fewer people will be prepared to work for very low wages but also because of existing minimum wage agreements which the trade unions will be willing to defend.

Incomes

After a long period during which the racial shares of personal income remained approximately constant, a substantial shift started in 1970 (when whites had about 70 per cent of total personal income). At present, their share is about 50 per cent and is dropping by about one per cent every year. Between 1985 and 1990, although average real income per capita dropped, it rose for all groups other than whites. And the All Media and Products Survey carried out in January 1993 indicated that between early 1991 and early 1992 black household incomes increased by 17 per cent in nominal terms, whereas the corresponding increase for white households was 10 per cent.

The most plausible interpretation one can put on these observations is that there has been a degree of wage compression over the past fifteen years, arising from more competitive conditions in the labour market and higher levels of black education. The net effect has been a decrease in relative inequality between all South African households taken together, but an increase in inequality among black households. A substantial number of black households continue to rely on low agricultural incomes and state transfers at the same time as a skilled working class and middle class is growing in black society. The trend towards greater equality among the population as a whole will continue. Reversal of the trend towards increased inequality among black households will require substantial progress against unemployment and poverty, for which a sustained economic growth rate of at least 3.5 per cent will be needed.

Development and policy issues

The political context

Certain aspects of a political transition towards democracy have implications for the economy. The first is *deradicalization* of a formerly excluded opposition; this may have to occur in a negotiated transition if innovative elements in a ruling coalition are to be able to outmanoeuvre their conservative colleagues and take the process of transition forward. One can point to a measure of deradicalization since the unbanning of the African National Congress and other political organizations in 1990. The prospect of a five-year Government of National Unity has promoted the search for convergence in economic policy positions. It has been suggested that what is now left of the ANC's economic programme is 'affirmative action plus anti-trust policy',[9] designed to improve the position of black people in the labour market and in the ownership and control of productive assets. Black business will seek a greater role for black-owned enterprises as well as a greater share of management and director positions within other firms. The Congress of South African Trade Unions, for its part, is proposing an ambitious restructuring of education and training which will help their members move up the occupational hierarchy. COSATU also believes that industrial policy should improve the quality of management, with a consequent impact on the productivity of workers.

In fact, other dimensions of economic policy will also be important. There are large unresolved issues about the ownership of agricultural land and about the siting and quality of new residential development, designed to cater for the increasing metropolitan and urban population. Also on the agenda will be policies to make the taxation and government expenditure package more sharply redistributive than at present.

The second aspect of political transition important for economic policy is the formation of economic *pacts*. The principal instrument for arriving at pacts is the sectoral forum, in which stakeholders negotiate the direction of future policies. A Central Witwatersrand Metropolitan Chamber has been in existence for over two years. More recent additions are a National Economic Forum, a National Housing Forum, a National Electrification Forum and a National Education and Training Forum, to name only a few of the more important. Progress is often slow; sometimes political actors stall the process for a considerable period. At the technical level, forums tend to get dispersed into a large number of working groups, dealing with particular aspects of policy. These can be hard to coordinate and sometimes crisis management takes priority over longer-term policy debate. The authority of forums varies; the Minister of Finance has successfully referred certain issues to the National Economic Forum for debate and resolution, while the Minister of Housing has recently been involved in a tussle over process and prerogatives with the National Housing Forum.

The third issue is that of *authoritative decision-making* by the state. For some time, a lame-duck government has found this difficult; changes in policy direction other than the abolition of discrimination have provoked charges of unilateral decision-making. The advent of the Transitional Executive Council and then a Government of National Unity may improve the capacity for delivering authoritative decisions, but this may happen rather slowly for two main reasons:

(1) The new government will be composed of parties of very different persuasion, and potentially subject to deadlock. In this respect the actual political composition of the new government will be important (see Chapter 2).

(2) There is a need to reconstruct second-tier government, which will be responsible for the delivery of most publicly provided goods and services. Regional governments will face fragmented administrative systems; the Northern Transvaal administration, for instance, will have to be put together from a part of the Transvaal Provincial

Administration and the administrations of Lebowa, Gazankulu and Venda. Vested interests mean that resistance to amalgamation of this sort is likely to emerge, making delivery in the short term more difficult. Tussles for power between centre and regions are likely to emerge, given that regional powers are to be exercised concurrently with parliament. Problems of 'cohabitation' in the French political sense will arise if some regional governments have different political majorities from the central government.

The necessity for structural adjustment
There has been much debate about the fate of commodity-exporting semi-developed countries, which have often industrialized behind high tariff and other barriers. One central issue is the medium- and long-term future for commodity prices. Recent experience has produced a degree of pessimism about both the gold price and other commodity prices. Gold will not regain the position it once had in the international monetary system and, in any case, South Africa is now a high-cost producer. (However, gold shares on the Johannesburg Stock Exchange increased substantially in 1993, indicating more bullish expectations.) Commodity prices are not expected to recover rapidly, in the short term because of limited growth prospects in the world's major economies and in the longer term because rising prices can be expected to induce resource-saving technical change.

These expectations encourage consideration of strategies designed to promote manufacturing exports. South Africa has not, on the whole, participated in the rapid recent growth in manufacturing exports, though there are exceptions in some fields. The government response in the late 1980s was to introduce a General Export Incentives Scheme (GEIS), which supports exports across the board. The scheme is to be phased out for good reasons: it is expensive, it often involves payments to enterprises which would have exported anyway, and its conformity to GATT rules is open to question.

Several options have been discussed in the South African debate:

(1) A trade liberalization policy, removing protection over a period of time, as part of a programme of cutting costs and becoming competitive in world markets. South Africa was asked to submit proposals to GATT for simplification and reduction of tariffs and other barriers for trade, and this was done recently after the

75

Minister of Finance had referred the matter to the National Economic Forum for debate. The successful conclusion of the GATT Uruguay round in December 1993 means that there will be even greater pressure on South Africa to liberalize.

(2) Selective assistance to sectors of manufacturing regarded as having high export potential if comparative advantage can be created by rapid learning and economies of scale.

(3) Building on South Africa's mineral exports base by exporting beneficiated (i.e. processed) rather than raw materials. Major projects in the production of aluminium and stainless steel are already under way with the help of special tax concessions.

(4) Promoting further industrialization by reallocating domestic demand to sectors believed to be of low import intensity (low-cost housing, basic consumer goods).

There are points to be made in respect of each of these positions. A general liberalization policy contains dangers in times of poor international economic performance. Intense competitive pressures may face some of South Africa's most labour-intensive industries (e.g. clothing) if tariffs are cut, worsening an already severe unemployment problem. The selective assistance route requires a state which can effectively 'govern the market' in the interests of economic efficiency. Whether the South African state can deal with the problems inherent in such a policy and make an economic success of it is open to serious question; it would involve the government having more knowledge than the private sector, as well as pursuing a more activist policy giving greater opportunities for industries to lobby for favoured treatment. Little attention has been paid to the failures of selective assistance policies. Beneficiation projects have required special taxation deals for viability, exacerbating future government revenue problems. And proponents of inward industrialization strategies tend to consider only the 'first round effects' of domestic demand reallocation; the full effects have greater implications for imports.

South Africa faces many of the same structural adjustment problems as a number of Latin American countries. It was integrated into the world economy in the nineteenth and early twentieth centuries by commodity exports, and its domestic industries have developed behind high tariff barriers. Industrial employment has developed to the point where trade unions have substantial effects on economic policy. The East Asian path to development, which has meant starting at the bottom of the manufactured product cycle and working up over time, is not available;

wages are too high for South Africa and comparable Latin American countries to start at the bottom of the product cycle. Rather awkward attempts have to be made to carve out niches in the middle of the cycle, in less buoyant international conditions than faced the successful East Asian countries in the 1960s and 1970s. The inefficiencies of the South African education and training system do not help.

Ownership and control of private enterprise

A related issue is that of the ownership and control of enterprises. A great deal of the private sector is controlled by an interlocking set of pyramids, at the apices of which are mining houses and insurance companies. Some of this concentration has been promoted by the system of exchange control in force for the past thirty years, making it difficult for South African companies to invest abroad. Concentration of ownership has also been a result of foreign sales of businesses in recent years.

It does not escape notice that these pyramids are directed mainly by white people, and the ANC has repeatedly stated that it intends to change the situation. Before 1990, nationalization was regarded as a key policy instrument. Emphasis has now shifted to affirmative action and competition policy. Both equity and efficiency arguments have been made in the debate. On the efficiency side, opinions differ: it is argued in favour of pyramided ownership that a few major shareholders can enforce accountability more effectively than many small shareholders. And powerful South African companies may be required to penetrate foreign markets, especially in mining. Others point to the discount at which holding company shares trade on the Johannesburg Stock Exchange as evidence that head offices subtract rather than add value to individual enterprises within a conglomerate.

In the end, broad-brush arguments such as these are only general guides. Changes in ownership and control take place all the time in response to changing market conditions. Stronger links with the international economy and the growth of new businesses can be expected to produce substantial change even without policy intervention.

There is widespread agreement that small and medium-sized enterprises should be promoted. A crucial question is whether or not the relationship between large and small enterprises is benign. This has to be considered in the light of changing theories about industrial organization. Some large enterprises have started to spin off parts of their operations into separate, smaller firms and to increase their procurement of inputs from small enterprises.

Changes in state revenue and expenditure
If the state is to play a useful role in development, its abuse as an engine of rapid personal accumulation of wealth for those in control of it must be terminated. This implies a greatly strengthened role for the public audit function, in terms of both traditional and performance auditing.

Given the goal of improving the investment performance of the economy, taxation must be designed to discourage consumption and encourage savings. This will mean a heavier but restructured burden on households. There will be particular pressure on the disposable income of upper- and middle-income households, already hit by declining pre-tax incomes.

Dilemmas will arise about taxation, and the policy outcomes are presently uncertain. The top rate of marginal taxation is 43 per cent, quite high by international standards, especially in the absence of a contributory social security system. Commodity taxes on goods in inelastic demand will result in the smallest efficiency losses; however, these may not meet equity requirements. An electricity tax might be considered, but since electricity is provided by the public sector (either directly by the Electricity Supply Commission, a parastatal corporation, or retailed through municipalities), it is more likely that cross-subsidization will be built in through new pricing policies, presently being negotiated in the National Electricity Forum. Property rates are likely to rise substantially. There may also be a payroll tax on the employment of graduates to help finance a tertiary education loan fund.

Most South African economists (including some, but not all, of the ANC's advisers) have warned that sharp increases in the aggregate tax burden are likely to lead to unsustainable efficiency losses. They are looking to the expenditure side of the budget in order to achieve greater, and better targeted, redistribution. Studies have found that the proportion of the state budget allocated to the various categories of social spending are in line with international averages, with the exception of direct transfers to pensioners, the disabled and children in need of support, on whom South African spending is low. The issue then becomes one of restructuring programmes, assuming expenditures not much higher than at present, to make them both more efficient and better targeted.

The role of the international financial institutions
Relations between the IMF, the World Bank and South Africa have been complicated by the length of the period of political negotiations. The

international financial institutions did not want to commence lending before the start of the transition, which might reasonably be dated either from the embodiment of the Kempton Park negotiations in legislation on 21 December 1993 or from the commencement of operation of the Transitional Executive Council on 7 December 1993. Both organizations did substantial preparatory work in their respective spheres – the IMF on macroeconomic balance issues and the World Bank on sectoral development issues, notably urban development, rural development and education. The first step was the negotiation of the already mentioned US$850 million loan with a five-year term, justified on the grounds of recent poor agricultural performance. Conditions associated with the loan appear to be minimal, though the government had to give some indications of its short- and medium-term economic policies. Considerable anxiety has been expressed by the ANC about conditionality, on the grounds that a new government might find itself under constraints imposed by the international financial institutions, in addition to those imposed on the ANC by its participation in a Government of National Unity. But the weak condition of South Africa's balance of payments may compel further and tougher negotiations with the IMF for support on other grounds.

World Bank analysis has reached the stage immediately preceding project formulation, at least in some fields. Work already undertaken has influenced the policy debate, but there is likely to be some delay in getting a government decision about priorities which will guide the selection of projects from a fairly large potential basket.

Furthermore, it is clear that South Africa needs technical assistance to bring development policies up to international best practice standards after a long period of isolation. What is less clear is whether South Africa has a major *financing* problem, as opposed to a *development* problem. To take an example: what constrains housing development is not so much the aggregate availability of loanable funds, nor the ability to develop new financing instruments (e.g. securitization of mortgages); it is rather the ability to retail end-user finance and to deal with the problems of risk and transaction costs at that level. More intangible issues sometimes enter the debate: perceptions of the cost of the increased policy leverage which comes with higher levels of lending and 'stamp of approval' effects of IMF and World Bank loans on private direct foreign investment have already been mentioned.

So the role of major lending (as opposed to relatively low-cost technical assistance) by the World Bank has to be carefully considered. At present, outstanding South African debt trades at between 2.5 and 3.5 per cent over London inter-bank offer rates (LIBOR), and the government and parastatal corporations expect to pay at least 2 per cent over LIBOR on new borrowing. Any substitution of World Bank financing for public lending on *foreign* commercial markets will bring down the cost of funds. Assessment of borrowing from the World Bank, to the extent it substitutes for borrowing on the *domestic* market, is a much more difficult and less clear-cut matter.

Conclusion: the way forward

Confidence in the South African economy has improved noticeably since April 1993. To some extent, this is a result of signs of slow recovery in the international economy, which is expected to work through to the South African economy with the usual six- to nine-month lag. Progress towards an interim constitutional settlement, after a difficult period following the collapse of the CODESA talks in mid-1992, has also helped. A third important factor has been the astute management of the economy by the Minister of Finance and the Government of the Reserve Bank. The 1993/94 budget appears to have been well-judged, and monetary policy has paid off in terms of a marked reduction in the rate of inflation. The Minister of Finance has also shown considerable skill in bringing in the ANC to help shape economic policy.

The most important factors in the immediate future will be the satisfactory tying-up of the interim constitution and its embodiment in legislation, the level of political violence and the quality of campaigning in the lead-up to the April elections. Unfavourable developments could have a sharp adverse effect on confidence and on short-term capital flows. It is important that no rise in the bank rate should be forced during this period. If there are no unfavourable social and political developments, the growth rate might well rise to 2.5 or 3 per cent in 1994, halting the decline in real per capita incomes since 1989.

It is possible to expect a degree of pragmatic cooperation between the main political parties on maintaining the conditions for economic recovery. The two chief potential difficulties will be severe conflict between elements in the Freedom Alliance on the one hand and the government on the other, and social confrontation beyond any political party's ability to control.

However, as electoral campaining starts, it is likely to be difficult to build much more consensus about developmental policies, especially those with substantial redistributive implications. Debate on the reconstruction programme is becoming more precise and some progress will be made in developing technical financial and economic analysis of options over the next few months. Not surprisingly, the expenditure side of proposals is better developed than the financing side. But what will be implemented will have to be hammered out in the initial part of the life of the Government of National Unity. At stake, of course, will be the roles of the state and of the market in development policy.

Crucial in the medium term will be the construction of new administrative capacity within the state. The changing of the guard at the top of the central civil service may be the least of the problems; rationalization of second- and third-tier authorities is likely to take considerably longer and will be a more messily contested process. The upshot is likely to be that new policies of *regulation* by central government will be easier to implement than direct *provision* at regional and local authority levels.

Even if the hazards identified are successfully negotiated, it is highly unlikely that sustained rapid growth will be achieved before the end of the decade. South Africa will be fortunate to reattain in 2000 the level of real per capita income it had in 1975: advanced industrial society status is not just around the corner.

Notes

1 South African Reserve Bank, *Quarterly Economic Bulletin*, September 1993; South African Chamber of Business, *Business Confidence Index*, October 1993.
2 South African Reserve Bank, op. cit.
3 Ibid.
4 Ibid.
5 Republic of South Africa, Department of Finance, *Normative Economic Model*, Pretoria, 1993.
6 M. Brown et al., *Platform for Investment*, no. 1, 1992 and no. 2, 1993, Johannesburg.
7 Republic of South Africa, Central Statistical Services, *Quarterly Bulletin of Statistics*, Pretoria, September 1993.
8 South African Reserve Bank, op. cit.
9 H. Adam and K. Moodley, *South Africa's Negotiated Revolution*, Cape Town: David Philip, 1992.

5

EDUCATION IN SOUTH AFRICA: MEANS AND ENDS

JAKES GERWEL

Negotiations and reconstruction

As the process of political negotiations in South Africa moves towards the April 1994 elections, the urgent need to devise plans for the reconstruction of key sectors of society becomes acute, and nowhere more so than in the field of education. This chapter will focus mainly on logistical and political aspects of the process of restructuring education.

The challenges of educational reconstruction are enormous, since effective schooling has virtually collapsed in large sectors of the system. While parts of the racially fragmented education system have highly developed infrastructure and quality provision, the schooling system for the majority of the population is characterized by neglect and underprovision, with crippling shortages in such basic areas as classrooms, libraries, laboratories and textbooks, together with an undersupply of qualified teachers. This discrepancy is graphically expressed in terms of the differential per capita spending on blacks and whites; for example, in 1987 R6.6 billion was spent on schooling 6.7 million pupils, with R2.6 billion of that money spent on fewer than a million white pupils and R2.5 billion on more than 4.7 million African pupils.[1]

The constitutional negotiations that began in 1990 were designed to achieve a redistribution of the political power that had hitherto been the monopoly of the white sector of the population. How to achieve the redistribution of access to social services and assets now becomes the major issue, both before and after the elections, for planners and policy-makers, including in the field of education. It is not, for example, as if the highly developed infrastructure of white schooling is simply available for sharing or reallocation; there are complex logistical and subjective factors acting as severe constraints on the process of recon-struction. At the same time the inequalities are so glaring, and the absolute degradation of schooling for the black majority (including Coloureds and Indians) so stark, that a programme rapidly to address the latter situation may, in the words of a draft paper by the Development Bank of South Africa, be viewed in its own right as a moral responsibility for the government and all the members of the community.[2]

The challenges of equity and development

Some understanding of the history of the engineering of educational inequality and hence of the destruction of the foundations of decent schooling is necessary for an appreciation of the extent of the educational crisis in South Africa. Indeed, apartheid South Africa may be unique in the way it deliberately planned for the educational underdevelopment of the human potential of its majority population and articulated its objectives. Apartheid education policy was not concerned with the provision of education as a basic human right to black people. Its aim was to produce a relatively low-skilled labour force and to reproduce the racially struc-tured division of labour and the unequal social and political structures necessary for securing the privileged position of the white community.

The dual role of Bantu education – first, as one factor in a specific form of capitalist development, and second, as one of the means of reproducing racial inequalities – resulted in a particularly exaggerated disparity in education provision between white and black at all levels of the system. It was this deep inequality which drove the resistance against apartheid and which today informs much of the impulse to define a new social order.

The indices of this systemic inequality are well documented. In dis-cussing how the years of neglect might be redressed, it is important to recognize how powerful is the sense of inequality and expectation of equalization in order to grasp the political complexities of reconstruc-tion. Reconstruction thinking often, and quite logically, argues for strate-gic human resource development on a relatively narrow base, privileging in the short term a relatively small – even if strategically crucial – elite. But it fails – again in the short term – to satisfy competing demands of mass society. Thus educational (and other) planners in South Africa have to engage simultaneously with issues of development and equal rights in order to strike a balance between these two poles which are inevitably in tension with each another.

Education as a human right to which all sectors of the populace have equal rights of access; investment in education as an imperative for social and economic development; and education as necessary for the establishment and consolidation of a democratic political order are three key factors that must govern educational reconstruction in South Africa.

The notion of 'society' in the sense of shared social definitions and a common moral discourse has been so severely eroded in South Africa that all projects of national reconstruction face the prior imperative of making explicit their underlying values and goals and of searching for their common acceptance. This is perhaps most vividly illustrated with reference to the law. The law, the legislature and the organs of enforcement have in the past been so blatantly used for discriminatory, exploitative, repressive and dehumanizing purposes that respect for and faith in the law have been fundamentally undermined. Thus shared acceptance of the social function of these organs has to be regained. Similarly with education: the collapse of the culture of learning and teaching is so pervasive that the process of educational reconstruction will have to begin with a search for and articulation of common goals and a shared commitment to the process of reconstruction.

The human rights approach underpins the argument for equalization and the stress on equity. This involves consideration of the level to which compulsory and/or free education is provided and the equalization of opportunities for access to various forms of higher education. The human rights approach, which in South Africa will in every respect have to address the historical withholding of rights, recognizes the phenomenon of massive adult illiteracy and the need for adult basic education. This raises the vexed question of costing, financing and affordability. Moves towards equalization in education in a society where government spending on education already exceeds 20 per cent of national budget (or 7 per cent of GDP) will have to involve a considerable reallocation of resources (with all the attendant political complications), as well as the diversification of sources of educational funding.

The poor performance of education has directly contributed to the poor performance of the South African economy, which suffers from a skills shortage and inadequate productive capacity on the part of the majority of the population. The ability of this majority to contribute to economic growth and development is severely constrained by a lack of access to education: it is calculated that 31 per cent of the total population aged 20 years and older are functionally illiterate, and that 1.8 million people are without any education at all.[3] In both these instances of educational disadvantagement the African population predominates.

Economic recovery and growth require investment in education and training for the rapid development of the technical, managerial and entrepreneurial skills of the historically disadvantaged majority. This investment would have to be at all levels of education and training: the access of blacks to higher education has to be dramatically accelerated as it is here that high-level human resource development occurs; the quality of basic education, particularly in the crucial areas of science, mathematics and technology, needs to be dramatically enhanced; the skilling of the existing workforce requires resources for adult basic education and industrial training.

An equally compelling motive for the reconstruction of education ensuring decent basic schooling for all, as well as real opportunities for access to higher and other forms of further education, is the need to enhance the conditions for the establishment and working of democracy. An educated population is one with improved ability to access information and to make informed public choices. Moreover, education is an important vehicle for the inculcation of attitudes of tolerance and respect for diversity.

There is broad agreement across virtually the whole political spectrum about the principles which are to underpin a future educational dispensation. It is agreed that education should be non-racial in organization and content; that the principle of non-sexism should operate at all levels; that there be a single system (allowing for regional and other variations); that there should be an integrated approach to education and training; that democratic participation of relevant stakeholders should be ensured and historical imbalances in respect of gender, race and other social factors redressed. As recently as 1991, there was still fierce argument about these principles; today they are broadly shared by the current government and the democratic movement. The crucial questions are how to move from the present racially fragmented and grossly uneven system to the one sketched above, and how specific educational content is to be given to those principles.

The principal actors

There are two main contending actors in this process of educational restructuring: the present South African government on the one hand, and the democratic movement on the other, with the private corporate sector, which has organized itself around educational and training initiatives, representing a third major role-player and stakeholder.

The South African government continues to control the current educational bureaucracies, effectively, therefore, remaining in charge of policy-making and implementation and of the delivery of educational services. Education is the responsibility of an overarching Department of National Education, three separate Departments of Education and Culture for whites, Indians and Coloureds, the Department of Education and Training for Africans, education departments in each of the six so-called Self-Governing Territories* and the four nominally independent homelands (TBVC).

There is little doubt that the democratic movement or liberation alliance – that is, primarily, the ANC and COSATU – will constitute the major part of a new government, incurring the final responsibility for educational reconstruction and effective delivery in terms of the anticipated new values and objectives. A new government will, however, be inheriting much of the current educational bureaucracy, personnel and delivery systems. How administrative systems and structures are changed and reallocation of resources is effected will, therefore, become a major *political issue*.

The policy and planning required can be effectively implemented only with the knowledge, information and capacity which accession to state power makes available. The current government departments have not, in the continued execution of their responsibilities for delivery, ceased all policy updating, adaptation or restructuring. On the contrary, in the three-and-a-half years since the start of the process of political and constitutional negotiations, government educational planners had been involved in major policy initiatives and have embarked on restructuring with the potential for significantly shaping the future system and constraining their successors. The most dramatic example in this context is the semi-privatization of white state schools, with public assets being distributed in favour of white communities. Another example is the large-scale early retirement of teachers in the white, Indian and Coloured sectors, ostensibly to address the over-supply of teachers as calculated on a separate racial basis. The newly established National Education and Training Forum (NETF) revealed that the government educational authorities had embarked on a new cycle of curriculum development, not only an enormously costly exercise but one whose products would apply for the next fifteen years.

It is now recognized that the earlier and rhetorical insistence on the

*Gazankulu, Kangwane, Kwandebele, KwaZulu, Lebowa and Quaqua.

government agreeing to a 'moratorium on all acts of unilateral restructuring' should have focused instead on how to arrive in this interim period at some partnership arrangement with the following objectives: (a) to prevent or minimize unilaterally conceived changes which might predetermine the future educational system in ways detrimental to the achievement of the new national goals; (b) at the same time to avoid a breakdown in the continuing process of delivery and provision; and (c) to employ the negotiation process (and developing modes of cooperation) to undertake the preparatory groundwork for the inevitable restructuring after the change of regime.

The National Education and Training Forum
The NETF could prove to be the key agency in this context. It is the latest in a series of forums established to provide for joint planning and decision-making in the social and economic reconstruction of South Africa (see Chapter 4). These forums represent one of the more tangible outcomes of the general climate of negotiations introduced by the start of constitutional talks between the major political actors.

An account of the efforts to get such a forum established for education is revealing about the political difficulties involved in changing the current educational dispensation. In 1991 the democratic movement attempted to persuade the South African government to include education on the national agenda as an item for negotiation alongside the political and constitutional issues. Following the disastrous results in the school-leaving examinations for African pupils at the end of 1990, ANC President Nelson Mandela brought together educationists representing a broad range of educational organizations and institutions, spanning the political divide, to meet with State President de Klerk and his education ministers. Top on their agenda was how to deal with the immediate crisis of insufficient delivery and provision in black schooling. This was, however, coupled to a demand for the establishment of a forum to consider how best to demolish the logic of apartheid planning in education. In spite of the establishment of a joint working group which met throughout 1991, not much was achieved in terms of short-term practical results or with regard to the establishment of restructuring mechanisms.

The government's reluctance to commit itself to the establishment of such a forum surfaced in a new set of discussions in 1992. In March the democratic movement organized a national education conference drawing together the widest possible range of educational actors outside government. The conference sought and reached agreement on the values to guide a future education system, on codes of recreating a culture of teaching and learning, and – most importantly – on the need to establish an education forum in which government could be engaged on future planning for change.

Initially, government spokespersons voiced agreement in principle with the idea of a forum, but then began to slow down the process for its establishment. It was only after the democratic movement and the organized private sector demonstrated common cause on this issue, followed by an escalation of public demonstration in support of a forum, that the government finally agreed to enter a steering committee for its establishment. The process of negotiating a founding agreement was itself tortuous and characterized by government obdurateness.[4]

Now that the forum has been established and has begun its work, what can be learned from the process thus far?

Given the overall climate of negotiations and the fact that forums like the important economic forum were already established and functioning, one is justified in seeking understanding of the government's tardiness in entering into a forum on educational restructuring.

A likely explanation is that government educational planners were reluctant to participate in a joint decision-making forum with binding powers prior to winning major concessions on forms of regional government at the constitutional negotiations. Thus in this period they were proceeding with administrative adjustments in anticipation of strong regional and local government control over education.

Socially, the transition from apartheid to a post-apartheid order means moving away from racial segregation and racially differentiated privileges. One must assume that as a new political dispensation is being negotiated, there will be attempts to safeguard as much as is possible or permissible of the former social privileges of the white sector, even if no longer on an overtly racial basis. Education has always been the one social area regarded as most sensitive to the 'own affairs'* approach and to culture-specific or community-based concerns. It is in this field that the most concerted efforts at retaining some form of particularism within the general integrationist thrust of the emerging new social and political order can be expected.

The government's reluctance to enter into an education forum where

---

*The distinction between 'general affairs' and 'own affairs' was at the heart of the legislative process enshrined in the tricameral constitution of 1984. It was an attempt, in effect, to give the Indian and Coloured minorities a degree of control over policy-making in certain specified areas.

policy changes could be jointly debated and decided upon coincided with the period in which – during the constitutional negotiations – arguments for stronger devolution of powers from central to regional government were advanced with greater force. At the time of writing it is still not clear exactly what powers will reside respectively with central, regional and local government, although the constitutional principle of substantial devolved powers has been established.

In his opening address to parliament in January 1993, President de Klerk made some pointed announcements about educational restructuring, giving a clear indication of government thinking. He announced the establishment of a transitional administration headed by a cabinet minister (now operating as the Education Coordinating Service, or ECS, directly under the Minister of National Education) and charged with coordinating the provision of education during the transitional phase, preparing new legislation on education and generally managing the entire process of change. The aim, he claimed, would be to complete – preferably by no later than 31 March 1994 – the process of rearranging and rationalizing the existing educational system into 'new executive regional departments'. Further, de Klerk stated that 'while moving away from the racial basis of education, differentiated education based on religious and cultural values and the mother tongue, with equal governmental support, will remain a right for those who desire it'.[5]

Differentiation is of course a characteristic of any educational system and is manifested in many ways within the same system; this must of necessity also apply to the future South African education system. The provision of different educational experiences for various pupils risks offering an education that is better for some than for others and thus reproducing inequity.[6] In the South African context, great caution has to be exercised to ensure that the linking of regional government control over education to religious, cultural and linguistic differentiation does not lead to the continuation in different guises of the current racially based inequities.

The relationship of the central state to the proposed regional governments is in another respect very important for educational progress in South Africa. Successful development and redress in the short to medium term require a strong state with the capacity to implement programmes through fiscal direction and the determination of national goals and objectives. Autonomous regional governments can significantly compromise the capacity of the future central state to fulfil this function.

The above argument demonstrates that the broad and rhetorical agreement on principles does not mean that there is equal agreement about how to implement these principles in terms of organization or educational content. However, the NETF has been established and it has been agreed that it will establish committees on restructuring to accompany the government's Education Coordinating Service in its process of rearrangement and rationalization as announced by the State President, and that it will note and take appropriate action with regard to any other restructuring exercises in the education departments.

The final section of this chapter examines some aspects of this novel relationship of the extra-governmental forces 'accompanying' – the word proposed by government – state agencies in their processes of restructuring.

Preparation for restructuring: immediate tasks

Systems integration is the most immediate task. A prerequisite for integrated and rationalized educational planning, budgeting and provision is the rapid coordination of the racially and politically fragmented system.

The benefits of such an integration would not be (as has long been the popular belief in anti-apartheid circles) direct savings on administrative personnel expenditure as a result of the abolition of duplicating bureaucracies; investigations have shown that South Africa, in spite of the illogicality of its administrative decentralization, is, in fact, not overspending on educational administrative personnel. The gains would be in the enhanced rationality of integrated planning and budgeting to provide a national overview of available resources and needs, and to ensure greater efficiency of delivery and more effective monitoring of outcomes.

The government's ECS administration is currently engaged in gathering and analysing information about the systems presently in place. It is comparing the various pieces of existing legislation for the provision of schooling, the different administrative and support systems, and the systems related to the provision of schooling. This information-gathering phase is a preparation for the planning of systems restructuring. It is this process in which the NETF is now involved, and through which the democratic movement and other extra-governmental agencies must seek to influence and shape the foundations of the future system being laid in this transitional period.

There is the real danger that a government in power will present the shared information as over-technical, obscuring the politics of educational organization and the so-called hidden curriculum. The NETF will have to negotiate access into the information-providing bureaucracy if it is to put the technical data into context and understand the particular form of organization being described as a function of a specific political project.

The democratic movement is at a distinct disadvantage with regard to material resources, technical infrastructure and available human capacity to maximize the opportunities offered by cooperation with the current state apparatus. The establishment of some minimum level of good faith is imperative for the success of the ensuing negotiations and it would not serve the process if the good faith of the government is continuously placed in question, or indeed vice versa. Some levelling of the playing-field – to resort to a topical phrase of contemporary South African political discussion – can, however, only be to the advantage of the process and the working relationships. It may be advisable for the NETF to ask for an international task force (possibly UNESCO) to monitor the process of restructuring as envisaged. International monitoring has become an accepted feature of the transition in South Africa, and in this particular case the task force would be combining a confidence-building function with the provision of expertise in a field that is highly technical and specialized.

The activities of the ECS are not the only restructuring functions with which the NETF will have to acquaint itself and become involved. The ECS specifically does not operate in areas of planning of the Department of National Education, and these include determining

the general policy to be applied with regard to formal, informal and non-formal education in respect of norms and standards for the financing of running and capital costs of education for all population groups, salaries and conditions of employment of staff, the professional registration of teachers, and norms and standards for syllabuses and examination and for certification of qualifications.[7]

These, in fact, are the crucial areas of educational planning to which prior access should be gained and in which the substantive changes to the education system will occur.

What the democratic movement has to gain from the opportunity of cooperation is an understanding of where the key or nodal points in the educational bureaucracy are. The politics of negotiations dictate that current personnel in the civil service will largely be inherited by the successor state. At the least, replacement of personnel in positions strategic to policy formulation and implementation will have to be negotiated.

Conclusion

The approach in this discussion may appear statist, with the emphasis on ways in which a 'government in waiting' prepares in cooperation with the current government for a transfer of responsibilities and a reform of institutions. This analysis has deliberately not dealt with either the substantive changes proposed by various actors or the participative and consultative processes which a democratic government will have to follow in reconstructing education. It is, however, urgently necessary for the democratic movement to begin thinking in these terms, understanding the political and administrative logistics of giving effect to the various policy options.

In a recent draft document on a policy model for human development from the Development Bank of South Africa, some of the concrete interventions required in education are itemized and precisely costed. The document mentions, for example, building some 75,000 classrooms to meet the existing backlog and to provide for the anticipated enrolment growth; upgrading some 50 per cent of existing classrooms; upgrading teacher training colleges; training new teachers at a rate of 15,000 per year to provide for both growth and a reduced pupil-teacher ratio; in-service training for some 50,000 existing primary school teachers; additional provision for teacher salaries owing to expanding numbers and higher qualifications; increased provision of books and other curricular supplies; improved provision for special education; development of pre-school 'educare' opportunities (catering for up to one million six-year-olds) so that children are better prepared for schooling.

In the field of adult education and training the document provides costing estimates for the sustained upgrading of existing technical colleges; a programme of basic skills training aimed at 1.9 million economically active persons aged between 20 and 40 with only primary education; an industrial training strategy as a negotiated partnership between government, employers and employees; an adult literacy programme for the economically active population between the ages of 20 and 40 with no education at all.

It is not, therefore, as if there is a total absence of plans, strategies and policy positions to draw upon. The democratic movement's National Education Policy Initiative (NEPI) report provides a broad framework for education policy evaluation; the Congress of South African Trade Unions has done substantial work on education and training policy; the ANC has commissioned its Centre for Education Policy Development to produce a comprehensive policy document; the Education Policy Units at the Universities of the Western Cape, the Witwatersrand, Natal, Durban-Westville and Fort Hare are all in one way or another contributing to policy development for the democratic movement.

The success of the educational policy of a democratic government will be affected by the nature of the preparatory work done in this short interregnum – hence the concentration in this chapter on the seemingly mundane subject of negotiations about bureaucracies and their workings. No allusion has been made to that massive challenge beyond the redress of material neglect: that is, the more subjective task of restoring the culture of learning and teaching which was so severely and extensively eroded through a combination of factors; or to the potential political volatility of heightened expectations in all fields, including education; or to the presence of strong conservative forces which would seek to resist and obstruct all forms of reconstruction towards non-racialism and greater equality. An adequate response to each of these challenges is conditional on effective access to and control of the policy, planning and delivery systems.

Notes

1 James Moulder, 'Education and distribution', in Robert Schrire (ed.), *Wealth or Poverty: Critical Choices for South Africa*, Cape Town: Oxford University Press, 1992, pp. 161–73. (The figures for 1987 are the latest audited ones available.)

2 Development Bank of South Africa, 'A macro-economic policy model for human development in South Africa', draft paper, p. 1 (see also Chapter 6, note 7).

3 Ibid., p. 5.

4 The author of this chapter was party to these negotiations.

5 Press release of State President F.W. de Klerk's opening address to Parliament, 29 January 1993.

6 See also National Education Policy Investigation, *The Framework Report and Final Report Summaries*, Cape Town: Oxford University Press, 1993, pp. 20–21.

7 See National Policy for General Education Affairs Act, Act 76 of 1984, of the Republic of South Africa, Section 2 (1).

6

HEALTH PROVISION IN A FUTURE SOUTH AFRICA

MICHAEL SAVAGE AND OLIVE SHISANA

Introduction

In its essence apartheid was a system of racially structured enforced inequality. As its legislative and administrative underpinnings are exposed and South Africa undergoes a transition to a democratic order, the ravages wrought by apartheid are brought into sharp focus. Democratization must entail reconstruction and a determined assault on the inequalities and the backlogs that disfigure and maim South African society. How that assault is to be mounted will be a critical issue facing the Government of National Unity after April 1994.

That the first phase of the transition towards democracy has coincided with the longest recession in the history of South Africa has imparted dangerous strains to the negotiation process, for distinct limits are placed on the scale of resources available for reconstruction. Extremes of poverty and wealth, long-festering grievances over structural racial inequalities in health, housing, education and other areas of basic need have now to be confronted within an economy that, in the assessment of *The Economist*, is 'prostrated' after decades of economic mismanagement.[1]

In three consecutive years since 1990 the economy has shown zero or negative growth and the prospects for any sustained growth are at best modest, as Chapter 4 has shown. The depth of the economic crisis in South Africa is reflected in its disastrous employment record. Currently it is estimated that 5 million people, some 46 per cent of the labour force, are without formal sector employment.[2] The number of formal sector jobs has virtually stopped expanding and fewer than one-tenth of new labour market entrants each year manage to find a job in that sector.[3]

The South African economy is malformed, damaged and ill-equipped to meet the depth of the problems that confront it. Currently it mated that 17 million people, or 42 per cent of all households, live b the stringently defined Minimum Living Level of R600 (approximal £109) per family per month.[4] Some four million of these people can b classified as ultra-poor; they are malnourished and face the danger of starvation. The extent of poverty in the rural areas is particularly marked, with some 80 per cent of households living below the minimum subsistence level.[5] The failure of the South African economy to provide for the basic needs of citizens is reflected in daily living conditions: 12 million people have no access to potable water, 18 million are without adequate sanitation and 23 million have no access to domestic electricity.[6]

The cost of providing water to 3.2 million urban homes and 1.6 million rural households is calculated to be R13 billion; providing 3.4 million urban units and 1.9 million rural households with sanitation would cost R600 million. Furthermore, the cost of providing electricity to 60 per cent of South African households is estimated to be R4.3 billion in capital and recurrent expenditures over five years. These calculations were based on a 'Macroeconomic Policy Model for Human Development in South Africa', prepared by the Development Bank of South Africa, the Kagiso Trust and the Independent Development Trust.[7] Without massive international aid, it is unlikely that South Africa will be able to provide basic needs for the majority of the disenfranchised, who naturally expect the installation of a new government to yield a better standard of living.

The grim fact is that South Africa is trapped into developmental stagnation, and there is no easy way forward in attempting to meet the basic needs of its citizens for healthy living conditions. As one commentator has noted, it is the peculiar characteristic of the current negotiated transition in South Africa that four basic problems have to be confronted simultaneously: stability, growth, redistribution and legitimacy. If a negotiated transition to a viable democratic future is to succeed, movement on all four fronts will be required.[8] Developmental policies and programmes cannot succeed unless concrete and measurable goals are set, and gains achieved, in at least three of these areas.

This chapter examines the extent of the task required to meet the health needs of the South African population. To provide primary health care services as a means of redressing the apartheid-generated inequities in access to health care is calculated to cost South Africa R3.2 billion over the next five years in recurrent spending and R875 million in capital expenditure.[9] This expenditure is over and above the R22 billion spent annually in providing health services in the private and public sectors. Although changes in existing patterns of social expenditures in health and a reorganization of the ways in which provision is made for the services are patently necessary, major improvements in the health status of the population will result primarily from wider development policies rather than from alterations to any existing arrangements within these areas. Much can be achieved through the improved utilization of existing resources, but major gains will depend upon development policies that provide for economic growth, redistribution, political stability and legitimacy, and which address the deep-seated inequalities that are embedded in existing social structures.

Current health care provision in South Africa

South African health care provision is in crisis. Existing health care services are so inefficient, inequitable and fragmented that they fail to meet basic needs of the population. A measure of this crisis is the fact that while South Africa allocates a relatively large proportion of its GNP to health care expenditure (some 6.4 per cent in 1989/90, which is greater than the World Health Organization's recommended 5 per cent for countries in a similar economic position[10]), many South Africans still lack access to basic health services. In its latest development report the World Bank states that South Africa's health status relative to income was one of the worst in the world. According to the report, 53 per cent of South African children aged between two and five suffered from stunting as a result of malnutrition.[11] This compared with an average of 39 per cent in the rest of Africa. The annual incidence of tuberculosis in South Africa (15 cases per 100,000 population, with 80,000 new cases annually) was 15 per cent above the average for Africa and more than ten times the rate of developed countries. Similarly, figures indicate that South Africa falls well behind poorer African countries in its immunization of children under one year against serious diseases. In 1990–91, 63 per cent of children younger than one received immunization against diptheria, whooping cough and tetanus. This compared with 89 per cent of Zimbabwean children and 79 per cent of Zambian children.

While serious issues concerning the equity, efficiency and allocation of health care resources require urgent attention by any new government, health service provision must be seen within a wider context. The quality of a nation's health is largely determined by its political and economic environment. Access to clean water, adequate food, housing, employment and sanitation play the decisive role in determining the health status of a population. While effective changes in health service provision will improve access to health care, long-term improvements in a national health status hinge on tangible improvements in the living conditions of the population.

The deficits of existing health services provide a set of pointers to tasks that will confront any future government in reshaping these services so as to better meet the needs of the population for adequate health care. These are outlined below.

First, *deep financial inequalities* exist within health services and require addressing. These mutually reinforcing inequalities are severe at several levels. Geographically, health care expenditure and provision are skewed towards the urban areas and away from the rural areas; although 30 per cent of the population live in self-governing (mostly rural) homelands, the state in 1990 spent R810 million on health in these regions (i.e., 10.4 per cent of state health expenditure). Per capita national expenditure on health services is biased towards whites (R597 per capita expenditure in contrast to R138 per capita for the African population); there are marked inequities in the financing of different levels of service, with the bulk of resources being allocated to tertiary-level care, while primary health care receives only some 5 per cent of national health care expenditure.[12] Such financial inequalities clearly reflect the priorities around which existing health services are organized.

Second, *the existing health services are deeply fragmented.* Until recent months there existed fourteen separate ministries of health (four ministries in the tricameral parliament and ten ministries in 'homeland' governments); coordination between them was minimal. In addition, there is considerable fragmentation in the organization of services, with weak referral chains between different levels of health care services, leading to the inappropriate use of hospital services and of health service personnel; often patients requiring minor treatment are sent to tertiary care centres.

Third, existing services are organized around the provision of *curative medicine and capital-intensive technology* at the expense of preventive medicine and primary health care. Current estimates indicate that only some 5.4 per cent of the health care budget is devoted to the promotion of good health,[13] with the consequence that South African medicine has become disease- and hospital-centred.

Fourth, there is *maldistribution of medical personnel.* Of the 24,619 registered doctors only 5.5 per cent practise in rural areas, where more than 40 per cent of the population reside. A total of 65 per cent of all doctors practise in metropolitan areas, 11 per cent in cities, 12 per cent in towns and 6 per cent in small towns.[14] Although the concentration of doctors in large urban areas is a worldwide phenomenon, this concentration is particularly marked in South Africa and provides a clear illustration of Hart's law: that the availability of good medical care tends to vary inversely with the need of the population served. As a result of this maldistribution, about 2,000 foreign doctors, many of whom come from other African states, are streaming in to fill the gap in rural areas.[15] The tragedy is that South Africa is quickly becoming the USA of Africa, draining the brains of poorer countries to work in areas which South African doctors find unattractive. Some suggest that financial incentives may induce South African doctors to work in underserved rural areas.

Fifth, there is a marked and growing *divide between public and private provision* of health services. The current trend towards the privatization of medicine has resulted in 63 per cent of all doctors active within the four provinces working in the private sector.[16] This sector services the 20 per cent of the population who are on medical aid or medical benefit schemes, together with those who can afford private health care. In essence, a private health care sector has grown up to provide for the needs of the 69 per cent of whites, 5 per cent of the African population and 30 per cent of the Coloured population who are on medical aid schemes, while the public health care sector provides for the bulk of the population.[17]

Sixth, South African health services have *weakly developed ancillary services*. In 1991 the number of registered nurses (67,843), enrolled nurses (72,484), health inspectors (2,471), dentists (3,768), dental therapists (141), optometrists (1,168) and pharmacists (8,171)[18] was so inadequate that the needs of the population could not be met. One crude measure of this is the fact that in the four African townships in Cape Town there is only one pharmacy, outside of public health care facilities, to serve the growing population. In addition, there is a severe shortage of institutions to serve the needs of the mentally ill, the disabled and the elderly.

None of these problems in the existing provision of health services is amenable to easy solution, and a new framework for the organization of health services is urgently required.

Emerging policy options for health service provision

Current debates about the future structure of health services have identified a number of clear policy options. Central to these debates are the issues of what role the state should play in the provision of health services and what part, if any, the private sector should have in funding and providing health care. At its extremes this debate is between those advocating the creation of a National Health Service which is comprehensive, provides equitable services for all and is the sole provider of health care, and those advocating a mixed system of state and private health care with a prominent role assigned to the private sector and with the state supplying basic health care services to the poor.

The Centre for Health Policy (a unit within the Medical School of the University of the Witwatersrand) has identified three major policy options, each with a number of possible variations, concerning the principles around which health services may be reorganized.[19] To these options a fourth may be added.

Option 1: Nationalize the private sector
This option would involve bringing all health facilities and personnel under state control. It is, however, unlikely to be attractive to any future government for two key reasons. First, it would greatly escalate the financial burden on the state in providing health care services, doubling, for example, the number of doctors to be paid by the state, and this at a time when demands on state revenue in constructing post-apartheid education and housing will be at their greatest. Second, it could lead to health personnel leaving the health service of the country rather than being compelled to work in the public sector, and it would open up the possibility of an unofficial private market in health emerging, thereby undermining public sector health services. In summary, it is an option that would be expensive both fiscally in absolute costs and politically in terms of the potential loss of trained personnel. South Africa is already losing medical doctors, and this option will only exacerbate the problem.

Option 2: Keep public and private sector provision separate
This option will allow for private care to continue to be provided for those who want and can afford it, while building up and reorganizing state health services. The option differs from a mere rationalization of the status quo in that it is associated with proposed measures to control the growth of the private sector by ensuring that the full costs of using it are borne by consumers. This would involve removing tax rebates for medical aid and passing on to the private sector the full costs of the training of all health personnel within it. Critics of this option maintain that it entrenches a two-tier system that could undermine an effective public

health care service. This option needs more investigation to determine its appropriateness.

Option 3: Centralize funding for both public and private providers
This option would lead to the creation of a National Health Insurance system, involving compulsory contributions from all involved in formal employment into a central fund, bearing in mind that 46 per cent of the economically active population are without a job in the formal sector. Money from this fund would provide for a basic package of health services for all citizens, who could turn either to the public sector or, on the basis of a capitation fee to general practitioners replacing 'fee-for-service', to the private sector for the supply of health services. The basic package of health services to be provided through health insurance would require careful definition, as would the costing of each element within it. Critics of this option claim that it would probably encourage the growth of the private sector and aggravate the problem of containing cost escalations within this sector. The central and critical issue of what would form the package of minimum services available to all has yet to be addressed in any detail by policy planners. The Medical Association of South Africa has attempted to provide preliminary information on the package of minimum services; while the business sector maintains that these should be determined through a priority-setting exercise and should depend on the availability of resources.

Option 4: Business sector option
Preliminary proposals are that although it is the state's responsibility to provide basic health services to the South African population, it is in the best interests of business viability that employers provide health care to their employees, families and the wider community. These proposals maintain that central government should concern itself only with health policy planning and allocation of finances, and should leave regional structures to develop regional policies and provide services within the broader national framework. To integrate the private sector into national health structures would require the business sector to be represented within national, regional and local decision-making structures.

The way forward
The options sketched out above succinctly encompass key elements of the emerging debate over two issues: the relationship between public and private provision of health care, and the role of private health care. While

most major political parties are agreed that a unified, national and comprehensive structure of health services is required, there are major divergences between those who wish to see a National Health Service emerge, akin to the British NHS or the Canadian system or single payer system, and those who see this either as not being possible or as not necessarily desirable.

The option of restructuring South Africa's health services around the creation of a National Health Insurance system (financing of health care) is likely to form the basis of a detailed policy investigation by a future government. Such an option envisages the continuation of a private sector but does not exclude the different future forms of a National Health Service. Analysts have pointed out that countries which have created a comprehensive tax-funded National Health Service have done so by initially creating a National Health Insurance system. The single exception to this is Cuba. Elsewhere the general pattern has been one where initially voluntary insurance schemes emerge, followed by the introduction of compulsory insurance for large sections of the population (such as all those in formal employment), with the state coming in to fill the gaps for the uninsured and only later creating a National Health Insurance system. South Africa's future in health care financing may well lie along this road, part of which it has already trodden, for it allows for a mix of public and private financing without excluding any future options that may include the dominant or exclusive state sector financing of health services. Unfortunately only a small section (20 per cent) of the population benefits from care provided through medical aid schemes; with such a large proportion of the population not employed in the formal sector, the success of this option remains to be seen.

Such a road forward will not appeal to all. The Pan Africanist Congress is committed to a state-owned national health service that is 'decentralized and de-bureaucratized'; the South African Communist Party to health care being 'free and the responsibility of the state'. Neither of these political movements favours the introduction of health insurance. ANC health policy proposals, however, do not exclude this option from emerging, within the framework of providing free essential health care for all, financed through tax revenues and by direct contributions to medical insurance.

The need for equitable allocation of health spending

There are few indications about policy directions that major political organizations may adopt in other important areas. In the area of state expenditure on health, there is an obvious requirement that this should not discriminate on grounds of race and that it should be used to promote health services which are both efficient and cost-effective. Current state spending is biased towards whites and allocated to the support of inefficient, fragmented services, often having little impact on the lives of those most in need of health care. The way in which state spending is allocated requires fundamental restructuring. At present, of the 82 per cent of health spending allocated to the non-homeland areas, 76 per cent goes to provincial administrations (which administer curative hospital-centred care that consumes 43 per cent of their budgets), 18 per cent to the Department of National Health and Population Development, 4 per cent to the tricameral parliamentary structures and only 2 per cent to local government.[20] As primary health care is mainly delivered at a local government level, it is clear that primary health care services are chronically underfunded. At the same time increased resources are being allocated to curative services and to hospital-level care, which have come under pressure as one consequence of the weaknesses in the delivery of primary and preventive health services.

Health expenditure should be carefully targeted if it is to be effective. Such targeting is not taking place and there is little rational basis to current patterns of expenditure. Policies for funding health in South Africa are generally not based on epidemiological data, but more on political and financial considerations. Financial and administrative factors need to be taken into account, but epidemiological evidence that shows areas where increased resources would yield maximum benefit is clearly an important factor in budgeting for equity in health. A poignant example is that of allocation of the health budget given differences in health indicators. The infant mortality rate among Africans was 52 per 1,000 live births in 1989, compared with 8.6 among whites during the same year;[21] yet, as will be seen, budget allocation for health did not take into account these differentials. Given that infant mortality rate is an indicator of the health and socioeconomic status of a community, one would expect the budget for health services to be allocated to respond to infant mortality rate differentials. As we saw earlier, the per capita expenditure for Africans was R138 in contrast to R597 for whites, showing an inverse relationship between the health of the community and the resources allocated to serve the needs of that community. Even the very meagre resources given to the African community are not targeted to its most important health problem, infant mortality.

One of the contributing factors to the inability of health planners to budget for health care on the basis of epidemiological data is that there are no nationally agreed health priorities in South Africa. This is partly because there is no nation yet, although it is slowly emerging at the Multi-Party Negotiating Council; but also, more importantly, because there is a dearth of adequately trained public health managers in the country. Adequate public health management would require skills in health economics, to enable managers to examine the cost-benefit analysis of spending money on tackling specific health problems, and to enable public health planners to develop appropriate formulae for allocating resources. Current initiatives in the Western Cape, Transvaal and Natal to develop public health training will go a long way towards addressing this critical shortage in appropriate health personnel. However, these initiatives are unlikely to produce results in time to enable the Government of National Unity to restructure health personnel through a massive infusion of appropriately trained people. Over the next five years they will play a major role.

Nevertheless, a future government will need to redirect expenditure if it is to build up primary health care services and provide improved services for rural dwellers and those in informal urban settlements. Greater emphasis will have to be placed on preventive health care measures through the reallocation of resources within the health care budget. There is little scope for increased funding of this budget by raising taxes or by increasing the deficit, nor is it likely that significant resources can be moved from other areas of social expenditure into health.[22] Setting a health budget and deciding on the priorities at the local, regional and national level will involve a series of invidious choices, if redistribution towards primary and preventive care is to be implemented effectively. Demands for fiscal justice will result in a marked reduction in health expenditures benefiting whites, and it is probable that efforts to target spending effectively will mean that expenditures on both tertiary-level services and services for well-established urban dwellers will have to decline. Tough and awkward decisions await any new government confronting the need to change the structures within which health services are provided.

The existing system of provision is breaking down. The medical aid scheme industry as a whole is currently estimated to have an actuarial deficit (i.e., the deficit is projected, not actual debt) of R18 billion, with net assets of R1 billion.[23] Medical aid costs are escalating at 25 per cent per year,[24] overcharging and over-servicing are widespread, and the schemes themselves now estimate that one-quarter of all claims made in

1993 will be fraudulent.[25] In the public sector a different malaise can be detected, with the widespread over-use of higher-level health care facilities and underuse of primary health care facilities, mainly because the latter are underdeveloped. There is an urgent need to find ways of allocating resources effectively, to services which are internally efficient and equitable and which ensure that public spending benefits the disadvantaged more than the advantaged.

Delivery of health care services .

In 1944 the Gluckman Commission of Inquiry into Health Services reported and provided a model of how a national health service could be shaped.[26] The report proposed an advanced and comprehensive plan for health services in South Africa, one that equalled and in some important respects outstripped the recommendations put forward by the later Beveridge report on which the British National Health Service was founded.

The Gluckman Commission advocated the creation of a National Health Service in which all personal health services would be supplied free of charge; the creation of a network of community health centres, with one centre for every 10,000–30,000 people, each centre being staffed by a team of medical workers that would include health visitors, dentists, nurses and doctors; further linked to these centres would be a network of general practice specialists and a referral chain that attached the centres to all levels of hospital services. The proposed scheme for health services was based on the provision of primary health care in the community and the training of scores of health visitors who would be concerned with basic health education and preventive medical work in their communities.

The major elements of the model of health care delivery as first proposed in the Gluckman report (whose recommendations were never implemented) are again attracting attention. The need for future health services to provide for primary and preventive health care within the community is widely accepted and some practical models of how this can be done in both urban and rural environments exist. How to give national emphasis to primary and preventive care, the costs involved and the personnel needed to do this all require detailed planning attention. South Africa is poorly equipped to engage in this. National and regional health statistics are fragmentary and incomplete (with basic statistics such as infant mortality rates for the African population being based on estimates and not reported cases), and the country has few trained health economists or planners. Against such a background it will be difficult to target services where they are most needed, or to plan for the required levels of technical and financial support of services at district or regional levels.

The experience of Zimbabwe in transforming its health care system and promoting the primary health care approach after independence in 1980 provides apposite lessons for post-apartheid South Africa.[27] This involved the integration of preventive and curative services and the development of several programmes designed to provide access to health care for those who were previously excluded. Rural health care centres were built, provincial and district hospitals and many rural clinics upgraded; the programme of immunization against the six major childhood infectious diseases was expanded; a diarrhoeal disease programme was introduced, based on the promotion of oral rehydration therapy; a National Nutrition Department responsible for nutrition education and surveillance and for supervision of a Children's Supplementary Feeding Programme was established; and a village health worker and traditional midwife training programme was undertaken. These interventions resulted in important gains, reflected in marked and immediate declines in the infant mortality rate, both nationally and in particular areas: it dropped from 120 per thousand in 1980 to 83 in 1982.

The institution of such national programmes (a combination of vertical, horizontal and structural changes) in South Africa would be likely to produce gains similar to those experienced by Zimbabwe. However, two important features were associated with the reform of the Zimbabwean health system that have significance for South Africa. First, these programmes required the immediate expansion of government expenditure on health: the Ministry of Health budget grew by some 44 per cent immediately after independence. Second, the gains were fragile and more clustered around mortality indicators than nutrition (quality of life) indicators. Both of these are salutary lessons, for it is doubtful that the South African health care budget could expand at this rate (unless supplemented by foreign contributions) and, as noted, the problems of redistributing it are complex. Likewise, the extent of malnutrition in South Africa – an estimated one-third of black, Coloured and Asian children below the age of 14 are underweight and stunted for their age – points to the difficulties that South Africa will share with Zimbabwe in attempting to improve its quality of life indicators.

Both selective and comprehensive primary health care strategies that focus on vertical and integrated horizontal development programmes will have to be implemented if the national health status is to improve. Many elements of the vertical programmes that would need to be delivered if national health status is to be improved can be identified: simple and improved pregnancy management, nutritional screening and food supplementation projects, diarrhoeal disease control, oral rehydration therapy, programmes concerned with sexually transmitted diseases, in particular with AIDS, and programmes targeted to meet the needs of particular groups (the elderly, children, the disabled). At South Africa's level of wealth and health, improved access to appropriate health care would substantially improve survival and quality of life.

Elements of the integrated horizontal development strategies, which form the basis for the success of vertical programmes, include political empowerment, better income, food security in the household, healthy housing, access to adequate water and sanitation, and better education, particularly for women. Without these structural changes in society, the benefits derived from vertical problems are likely to be temporary.

AIDS: a health problem of the future

New problems await the health services, which are already overburdened with patients suffering from preventable diseases. One problem needs to be singled out, for its potentially profound and even devastating impact on health services, and that is AIDS. Estimates are that by March 1993 more than 43,000 people in South Africa were infected with the human immunodeficiency virus (HIV). Since 1982 more than 1,500 people have been diagnosed with AIDS, of whom 475 have died.[28] Although the first group of people to be affected were homosexuals, today HIV in South Africa affects more heterosexuals than homosexuals. It is spreading among people of all race-groups and much faster in those aged between 15 and 34 years, particularly pregnant women. The epidemic is spreading more rapidly in some areas than in others. Places that have been ravaged by war, such as Natal, are particularly badly affected. For example, HIV infection is ten times more common in Natal than in the Cape province; the prevalence of HIV infections in Natal during 1991 was 2.87 per cent but only 0.37 per cent in the Cape.[29]

The most reliable current projections are that between 15 and 27 per cent of the total adult population will be HIV positive within 20 years.[30] These figures, derived from a cautious projection model attracting international acceptance, suggest that South Africa soon will be facing the burden of vast increases in illnesses and deaths associated with HIV/AIDS. The economic costs of this epidemic will be substantial but in the short term (in the next 15 years) could probably be sustained in terms of the direct impact on the GNP. But although initially the order of total health expenditure that will be needed for the basic care of people with HIV/AIDS will be small, it is likely to become unsustainable beyond 1998. Between 19 and 31 per cent of total health resources are projected as being required for HIV/AIDS care by 1998, assuming that care continues to be provided in a more individualistic clinical way, with no attempt to shift to primary health care. This order of expenditure is set to have a drastic impact on the ability of health services to restructure themselves and will present a further uncharted challenge to the provision of adequate health care services in the future South Africa.

The AIDS epidemic in South Africa has caught the attention of politicians. They made an early decision that AIDS was such a major public health problem that political differences should not hinder the development of national strategies to reduce the spread of the virus. The National AIDS Convention of South Africa (NACOSA) was founded in October 1992 as a result of groundwork on the part of the ANC Health Secretariat and the South African Department of Health and Population Development specifically to develop a national strategy to halt the spread of AIDS.[31] This initiative has shown that it is possible to bring together groups on a non-partisan basis to tackle major public health problems that threaten to consume the resources for health service delivery. In spite of this noble effort by NACOSA, the challenge is really to develop intervention strategies that would encourage people to change to safer sexual practices. Judging by the descriptive nature of research studies on AIDS conducted in South Africa, and the dearth of intervention studies, NACOSA is unlikely to have a large menu of intervention strategies to choose from.

Conclusions

Among many problems that the new government will have to deal with a few are outlined below. As South Africa moves to restructure itself towards a system with federal features, where provinces will have some legislative and fiscal responsibility, coupled with functions to deliver social and health services, the challenge for health planning will be daunting. The nine provinces* designated in the interim constitution differ markedly in socioeconomic status, including indicators such as

*The nine provinces are: Natal, Northern Cape, Northern Transvaal, North-West, Eastern Cape, Eastern Transvaal, Orange Free State, Pretoria-Witwatersrand-Vereeniging and Western Cape.

infant mortality rate, access to water, sanitation and electricity, and illiteracy rate. The provinces also differ strikingly in their institutional infrastructure and administrative capacity to deliver health services effectively to their residents. Even within each province there are major disparities in access to these basic facilities, particularly between rural, peri-urban and urban areas.[32] The challenge will be for the new central government to plan and allocate resources to institute development strategies that will be implemented in all these different provinces with their different sets of problems. Given the political pressure for less interference from the central government, it is likely that the new government will find difficulty in meeting the expectations for access to better health care or to basic facilities. There is a possibility of huge migration from poorer to richer provinces. A glimpse of what awaits South Africa was seen when communities with resources were unwilling to have their areas demarcated into the poorer provinces. The poorer provinces are likely to be welfare states, depending more on fiscal transfers from the central government. Because of this carrot they may be more likely to implement national policies. The provinces with more resources are likely to pursue their own agendas. All these initiatives will depend on finalizing the new constitution. Much will also depend on how far the new South African state moves towards a federal structure with certain powers and functions devolved to the provinces (see Chapter 2).

Other issues that are likely to face the new government include the integration of marginalized young people into the public health sector. The young can play a very important role in improving health service delivery in communities, and the National Youth Development Forum has adopted a plan prepared by a technical committee to integrate 10,000 of them into the public health sector. This plan requires the training and education of young people while they provide primary health care services to the underserved in the rural and peri-urban areas of the country. They are to be trained through entry-level courses in specific areas, including community health, epidemiology, mental health, community rehabilitation, pharmacy, laboratory techniques, community safety and development. Armed with these skills, these young people are likely to provide community-based health care, focusing more on programme development and implementation. The resources required by the government will amount to R144 million, representing an increase of less than 1.5 per cent in the public sector health budget. This is considered to be the most cost-effective way of financing the increase in service provision that the country needs, especially in underserved areas.[33]

Finally, the new government will be faced with developing new strategies for halting the spread of AIDS, particularly in the war-torn areas. Since very few resources have been spent on statutory research on health compared with other sectors, the new government faces a major task in channelling resources into this area.

In the health field, the ravages wrought by past policies are considerable. A post-apartheid South Africa will inherit a daunting array of challenges in attempting to meet the needs of its citizens. Although there will be considerable constraints on the extent to which these needs can be met, notably those associated with having to repair a severely damaged economy, steps towards creating equitable health services are urgently needed. To predict how effectively South Africa will meet these needs is not easy; but it is certain that hard, creative tasks lie ahead.

Notes

The authors thank Dr Merrick Zwarenstein for his valuable and critical comments.

1 'A survey of South Africa: the final lap', *The Economist*, 20–26 March 1993.
2 *The Star*, 23 August 1993, citing the Annual Report of the South African Reserve Bank.
3 See André Roux, 'Options for employment creation', in Peter Moll, Nicoli Natrass and Lieb Loots (eds), *Redistribution: How Can it Work in South Africa?*, Cape Town: David Philip, 1991, pp. 101–17.
4 Andrew R. Donaldson, 'Basic needs and social policy', in Merle Lipton and Charles Simkins (eds), *State and Market*, Johannesburg: University of the Witwatersrand Press, 1993, pp. 271–320.
5 Francis Wilson and Mamphela Ramphele, *Uprooting Poverty: The South African Challenge*, Cape Town: David Philip, 1989.
6 'Independent Development Trust: a survey', *Financial Mail*, 21 May 1993, p. 10.
7 *Finance Week*, 23–29 September 1993, pp. 11–12.
8 F. van Zyl Slabbert, 'Reconstructing the state', *DSA in Depth*, August/ September 1993, p. 5.
9 *Finance Week*, op. cit.
10 Department of National Health and Population Development, *Health Trends in South Africa*, February 1991.
11 World Bank, *World Development Report: Investing in Health*, New York: Oxford University Press, 1993.
12 D.E. McIntyre, R.E. Dorrington, *Trends in South African Health Care Expenditure 1971–1988*, Occasional publication, Health Economics Unit, University of Cape Town, 1989.

13 Ibid.
14 P.N. Pillay, 'The distribution of medical manpower and health care facilities in South Africa', Carnegie Conference Paper no. 167, University of Cape Town, 1984.
15 South African Medical Journal editorial, vol. 83, no. 9, September 1993.
16 Medical Association of South Africa, 'Towards an integrated strategy for positioning the medical profession in a changing South Africa', 27/28 May 1993.
17 *Trends in South African Health Care Expenditure*, op. cit.
18 Department of National Health and Population Development, 'Registered manpower per geographic region in the RSA, 1991/92'.
19 Centre for Health Policy, 'The national health service and the future of the private sector – the case for national insurance', *Critical Health*, 1991, vol. 39, pp. 42–9.
20 Nicoli Natrass and André Roux, 'Making welfare spending work', in P. Moll, N. Natrass and L. Loots, op. cit., pp. 86–100, citing D. McIntyre.
21 Henry J. Kaiser Family Foundation, *Changing Health in South Africa: Towards New Perspectives in Research*, November 1991, Menlo Park, California.
22 On restraints on redistribution see Servaas van der Berg, 'Redirecting government expenditure', in P. Moll, N. Natrass and L. Loots (eds), op. cit., pp. 78–80.
23 I.J. v. H. Fourie, 'An employer's health care strategy in a transitional South Africa', unpublished paper, June 1993.
24 See Leon Lewis, 'Health care – a major crisis looms', *Affordability*, vol. 2, no. 1, 1992, pp. 8–9.
25 Mike Ellis, 'Health care critically ill', *Sunday Times*, 11 April 1993.
26 Union of South Africa: National Health Services Commission, 'The provision of an organised National Health Service for all sections of the people of the Union of South Africa, 1942–1944'.
27 Rob Davies and David Sanders, 'Economic strategies, adjustment and health policy: Issues in sub-Saharan Africa for the 1990's', *Transformation*, no. 21, 1993, pp. 78–93. Also David Sanders, 'Equity in health: Zimbabwe nine years on', *Journal of Social Development*, vol. 5, no. 1, 1990, pp. 5–22.
28 AIDS statistics printed in the *South African Journal of Infectious Diseases*, vol. 8, no. 1, 1993, p. 28, as reported by the South African Department of National Health and Population Development.
29 Paper presented by Q.A. Karim at the opening of the NACOSA conference on 22 October 1992 in Johannesburg.
30 Centre for Health Policy, *AIDS in South Africa: The Demographic and Economic Implications*, Johannesburg: Centre for Health Policy Paper, no. 23, 1993.

31 M. Steinberg, 'NACOSA. AIDS Bulletin', Medical Research Council, December 1992, vol. 1(2), pp. 12–13.

32 'Report on further work on the Demarcation/Delimitation of States/ Provinces/Regions (SPRs) Tabled at the Multiple-Party Negotiating Council on October 15 1993'.

33 This is based on the research work carried out by the Community Agency for Social Enquiry (CASE) for the Joint Enrichment Programme Project on behalf of the Marginalized Youth Conference.

7

CONCLUSION

J.E. SPENCE

This volume of essays has attempted to strike a balance between analysis of current developments in South Africa and future prospects for a newly installed Government of National Unity and Reconstruction following national and provincial elections on 27 April 1994. Throughout, the contributors have tried to focus on a moving target, given the rapid pace of events during the past twelve months. Yet we remain convinced that an understanding of events since President de Klerk's dramatic initiative of 2 February 1990 is essential to make sense of whatever happens in the years ahead.

It must be stressed that this study makes no pretence at being comprehensive in its treatment of South Africa's preoccupations: space constraints prevented any detailed discussion of such topics as housing, local government reform and the land question. This is not to deny their importance as areas of public concern. Rather, by inviting contributions on health and education, the editor sought to provide two major examples of the social agenda confronting a post-apartheid government. Indeed, it could be argued that education has a particular claim if only because – as Professor Gerwel clearly demonstrates – the National Party government, over a forty-year period, blatantly used education policy as an instrument for social control, designed to maintain white supremacy at the expense of black aspirations to benefit from the fruits of modernization. It is significant, too, that the challenge from young blacks to the might of the South African state during the Soweto revolt of 1976 – the violent prelude to the current drama – was the product of deep-seated resentment against the policy of Bantu education.

The new government – as the contributors to this volume have emphasized – will face hard choices. It will have to deal with great expectations of improvement in the quality of life for the deprived black majority. Its coalition structure, at least during the first five years, will make for cumbersome decision-making in which compromise will be essential. Indeed one must hope on occasion for different 'winners' and 'losers', as politicians decide their priorities and implement them in practice. The worst outcome in this context will be the emergence of a permanently aggrieved coalition of losers within both government and the body politic at large. What will therefore be required is an immense commitment to public education, one that involves persuading the electorate that the goals of reconstruction cannot be achieved overnight. As Nelson Mandela explained to the ANC Youth League in mid-January 1994, 'it is our task to explain to the people not to have exaggerated expectations'.[1]

Nonetheless, external observers must be wary of being patronizing: many South Africans, no doubt, recognize the force of the dictum *plus ça change* ..., but it will be the primary task of their government to provide clear evidence that the daily lives of the black population are being changed for the better, however haphazard the process may prove to be.

Finally with respect to external responses, the editor's judgment that South Africa will in time become 'just another country' may seem harsh. This is not to deny that the Western powers, for example, have important economic and political interests in South Africa and its region, and these will certainly persist under the new post-apartheid regime. There is also the possibility of external assistance in finding appropriate solutions for some of the structural problems facing the new government. William Gutteridge, for example, cites the need for 'international supervision and monitoring' (p. 62) with respect to military reform, while Jakes Gerwel argues for an 'international task force ... to monitor the process of [educational] restructuring' (p. 91). Similarly, Charles Simkins's observations on the role of the IMF and the World Bank (p. 79) have obvious relevance. Indeed, at a more general level it could be argued that South Africa's professional classes – soldiers, educators, doctors and academics, for example – can only benefit from contact with the outside world to make up for their relative exclusion from best practice during the sanctions phase. Thus the international community, to paraphrase Walter Bagehot, might well in this context 'advise, warn and be consulted'.

In the final analysis, however, the new government of South Africa will have to acknowledge that it is peculiarly on its own, that it cannot expect external actors to rescue it from political and economic disaster should that be the ultimate outcome. True, the UN and other external agencies will be sending some 2,800 observers to monitor the 1994 elections. True, the country will retain its fascination for the media and those academics interested in the theory and practice of state transformation. But what ultimately requires recognition by South Africa's rulers is that, following the demise of apartheid, governments and multinational companies will protect and enhance their interests not because of historical or traditional linkages, but on the basis of hard economic and political self-interest and the strength of competing claims elsewhere. And in a disorderly world there are plenty of those, ranging from the Bosnian tragedy to the economic attraction of China and the 'new tigers' of the Asia-Pacific Rim.

Nevertheless, despite the many qualifications of the analysis, there are grounds for cautious optimism. There is much to be done and the stakes are high, but the memory of past injustice and gross political error may just be enough to concentrate South African minds on the rewards that could attend the end of apartheid.

Notes
1 Alec Russell, 'Mandela warning as ANC unveils plan to rebuild South Africa', *The Daily Telegraph*, 15 January 1994.